D1400773

TOM RADEMACHER

Splitting Wood

Stories by
Michigan Columnist Tom Rademacher
First Place – National Society of Newspaper Columnists

Published by
Lake Michigan Books

in cooperation with
The Grand Rapids Press

Copyright 2009 Lake Michigan Books and The Grand Rapids Press
Published by Lake Michigan Books, November 2009

All rights reserved.
No part of this book may be reproduced in any form or by any electronic
or mechanical means, including information storage and retrieval systems,
without permission in writing from the publisher, except by a reviewer
who may quote brief passages.

Lake Michigan Books
P.O. Box 226
Rockford, Michigan 49341

Publisher's Note: These stories originally appeared in The Grand Rapids Press
between 1988 and 2009, inclusive.
All rights reserved. Reprinted with permission.

ISBN 978-0-9843392-0-4

Library of Congress Number: 2009911871
Printed in the United States of America

This book is dedicated to
Thomas F. and Patricia C. Rademacher,
who taught me the power of words

And to
The past and present employees of The Grand Rapids Press

And to
My family, who endured all the indignities
of living with a newspaper columnist

Santa Claus Girls
Grand Rapids Michigan

A portion of proceeds from this book
will be donated to the **Santa Claus Girls**,
a Grand Rapids Press-sponsored organization
who sees to it that no child in Kent County
be without a gift at Christmas.

For more information on this worthy non-profit corporation
that depends solely on volunteers
and sends 97 cents of every dollar it raises
to cheer young hearts, **visit santaclausgirls.org**

TOM RADEMACHER

SplittingWood

Table of Contents

Introduction

Some people think I wrote a newspaper column for a living.

In truth, I split wood those 20-odd years.

As a columnist, it's my job to fell trees, strip away the bark, and unveil the true essence of people, knots and all. Like working a woodpile of oak or maple, it's not always easy. But the results can render some incredible glimpses into the nature of men and women.

For the sake of a story, I have run the Boston Marathon, covered the Pistons and the Lakers at the Forum, bicycled the Canadian Rockies, roamed Tijuana, even jumped out of an airplane.

I've been privileged to report on the gritty underbelly of the homeless, on parents enduring their worst nightmares, of beggars and big shots and scoundrels. I have seen more dead bodies than a person should, been bamboozled and lied to, been witness to miracles.

But the best stories I ever rushed back to the newsroom with were of everyday people gutting it out in everyday ways, both rejoicing in and battling back against life's curves. You hardly ever read of them in check-out magazines. But The Grand Rapids Press – which gave me the only full-time job I ever had – has always found room, giving them dignity and a voice.

This book is more than a compilation of columns. It's testament to you, "the guy next door." It's women still hanging wash out on the line, men carrying beat-up lunch buckets to jobs that render no glory, kids gaining against all odds, faithful dogs, couples dancing in their kitchens.

I wielded the ax. But these stories are your stories.

Tom Rademacher

Foreword

I've never forgotten the frail image of Mazie Boogerd.

Most people lucky enough to be at Gerald R. Ford International Airport that spring afternoon trained their gaze upward, not at Mazie.

A Blue Angel fighter jet, on a rare stopover in West Michigan, had departed moments earlier when the pilot suddenly banked hard and roared back toward the airport. Afterburners are deafening at nearly 600 miles per hours, and the surprised onlookers cheered as the pilot tipped the jet's wings as if to wave, then snapped upward in a vertical ascent into the cloudless blue sky.

Most of those watching the thundering display would not have seen the ailing woman in her husband's arms, waving back. I didn't. I wasn't even at the airport that day. I learned about Mazie from Tom Rademacher, on the front page of The Grand Rapids Press. I won't spoil the end of the story here. For that, you'll have to read this book.

For more than 20 years, three times a week, Tom has been sharing his columns in The Press about our lives and our community by training his gaze where most people don't. It is hard work to write well, even more so to make it appear effortless, and over the years Tom has provided us countless glimpses into the human condition.

I first met Tom when I was a green reporter fresh out of college. To me, he was the seasoned veteran, a pro who'd just co-authored a series about wasteful spending at a local institution. I was impressed. It would not be the last time. Our careers would take different paths. I eventually moved into newsroom management. Tom was chosen to replace longtime Press columnist Tom LaBelle.

Many times, we would work together. (Every writer needs an editor!) So when Tom asked me to write the foreword for this, his first book of columns, I thought, "Ah, as an editor I usually have the last word. Now I get to have the first!" Then reality set in. How do you summarize a body of work that spans more than 3,000 columns? How does one convey how he became the writer most callers request when they have a story to share? How do you characterize a style of interviewing that unfolds its subject, drawing out details so fine that it can feel like you are there?

Mazie is that way for me. And so is the lasting image of David Schultheiss, the mentally challenged man who throws out the first pitch each Little League season at Riverside Park. And a little girl whose quest for a new purse made people consider what's really important in everyday life.

For faithful readers, it should come as no surprise to learn Tom's favorite novel is John Steinbeck's "The Grapes of Wrath." It's about ordinary people who are in fact extraordinary. So too, are many of the people Tom has introduced to us all. It's for that reason that the National Society of Newspaper Columnists honored Tom recently, giving him its top national award in the general interest category among columnists from the country's largest newspapers.

At a gathering recently to honor colleagues who had chosen new paths, my turn came to say a few words on Tom's behalf. I swallowed hard, and finally said, "There are no words."

I was wrong, of course. They are in this book.

John Barnes
Metro Editor | The Grand Rapids Press
Nov. 9, 2009

CHAPTER 1

Life

The Kingdom of Kindergarten

If you're like me, you missed "Write A Letter To Your Kid Day," which was celebrated earlier this month. I say it's never too late. So I penned this, bowing to third-person form, and suspect it's better than nothing . . .

Once upon a time, there was a little boy named Andrew who convinced his daddy that, since daddies hardly ever accompanied the little boy's kindergarten class on field trips, he should go. Daddy, daddy, puh-leeez.

The daddy started to say that he already knew everything he needed to know about kindergarten. For one, he had actually passed kindergarten. And for another, he had student-taught a kindergarten class while in college.

But when he saw the plaintive look in the little boy's eye, and coupled it with the realization that field trips should, indeed, solicit and make use of daddies, the daddy said OK.

They rode a bus, a big yellow bus teeming with screaming kids. And along the way to the grocery store, Good Queen Kim of Zuidema implored all her royal subjects to find not only their favorite brands, but also to locate the prices on those boxes of cereal and yogurt and toothpaste.

The daddy was placed in charge of his own son and three other subjects – Sir Nick, Sir Chester and Sir Kevin S., who, by Zeus, is not to be confused with Sir Kevin A.

While filing out of the bus, the good queen instructed all the mommies and the daddy to, above all else, not lose their kids. Which the daddy did immediately, just this side of the Coke display.

After rounding everyone up, they moved like a herd of sheep into a back room, where the manager of the supermarket explained how returned bottles and cans are boxed and stored. The daddy eyed the hi-lo in a corner of the room, and considered asking if he could drive it home but held his tongue.

They spread out after that in groups, their knightly mission being to decipher brands and prices. Each child held a clipboard, some for the first time, which, the daddy mused later, explained why every 22 seconds a child asked him, "Sire, can you hold my clipboard for me?"

"Life is full of difficulties," he heard himself say, against the commotion of fingers caught in the clips and pencils flung from the clipboards' holders.

Each young knave in the daddy's group had 40 cents to spend on a doughnut. And this they did prior to completing their task at hand, which resulted in the clipboards taking on the sordid textures of chocolate frosting and whipped cream and yellow custard.

Not one of the four could finish their doughnuts, causing the daddy to look for a receptacle, and finding none, quietly put the wads of pastry among some packaged produce, with plans to retrieve it later.

The Queen noticed this, and casually questioned the daddy, and the daddy realized that maybe he needed a refresher course in kindergarten himself.

But Good Queen Kim went off to check on her other subjects, and the daddy and his brood wandered off to record the prices of gruel.

Later, on their way to the yogurt section, they passed the mommy and daddy section and the daddy heard his young charges say:

"Budweiser!"

"Bud Light!"

"Yeah. Gimme a Bud Light!"

And the daddy cringed to think that television was upon the land.

As they walked the aisles to visit the cracker section, one kindergartner said, "I gotta go to the bathroom."

"Me, too," said the next in line.

"Me, too," said the third.

"Um," went the fourth, and then he whispered, "I don't know if I do or not. I better try."

The daddy collected their clipboards and off they went. And when they all returned, he meant to lead them to a new land in the store, but stopped, and announced, "Now I gotta go," and he had them wait by the frozen chickens.

Before leaving, they found themselves holding hands and skipping in untied shoes and they lost most their pencils and learned things like "My grandpa puts ketchup on his ice cream."

They rode the big yellow bus home a little taller, a little prouder.

And when the daddy put his tired kindergartner to bed that night and asked him what the best part of the field trip was, he answered, "The donuts – and being with you."

And the daddy dreamed the dreams of kings.

The End.

Sucking Up

Baseball cards? Marbles? Video games? Mere dust mites in the odyssey of life. Meet Morgan Wilburn. Age 7. Collects vacuum cleaners.

You name it – uprights, hand-helds, canisters, wet-drys – Morgan's got one. At last count, his stash stood at two dozen units.

And Friday, this little rug rat from Virginia created national headlines when he made a pilgrimage here to his mecca for all things vacuous:

Bissell Inc.

The Grand Rapids-based firm gave him the red carpet treatment, including first-class airfare, two nights' stay at the Amway Grand Plaza Hotel, limo service and a tour of the Bissell plant at 2345 Walker Ave. NW, where he schmoozed with mucky-mucks.

"I might work here someday," said the 62-pound prodigy, who also enjoys T-ball, gymnastics and is a card-carrying member of Cub Scout Den No. 1, Pack 13, in his hometown of Salem, Va.

Morgan, who was accompanied here by his 2-year-old sister, Bailey – she couldn't care less about vacuums – and parents, Julie and Guy, floored Bissell brass with his knowledge of everything from uprights to steam cleaners.

"He could design them, manufacture them and sell them," said David Kagan, Bissell's director of communications.

"He's a one-man band in the floor care industry."

After touring the Bissell plant, Morgan was ushered into a large room – carpeted, of course – that housed a welcome poster, balloons, and to Morgan's extreme liking, many, many Bissell products.

He uttered what you might expect from a second-grader.

"Wow."

But the presence of an older child took over from there. He scooted around the floor in his brown corduroys, testing some 20 vacuums and carpet sweepers. He plugged them in. He experimented with attachments. He flirted with hoses, variable switches, convertible designs.

"Ya got some stains?" he asked.

Yes they did, and someone sloshed a bottle of cola onto a carpet sample. Morgan went back and forth across it with a Bissell Big Green Power Brush. He nodded, as if to say, "Not bad."

Morgan's mother, Julie, stood by. She said she's not sure what tripped her son's fascination for vacuums. He received a toy vacuum as an infant, but she's not sure that provoked it.

"At first, I thought it was a better idea than the Power Rangers," she says. "Vacuums aren't violent. But then he wanted bigger and better vacuums.

"On Sundays, he goes through the newspaper, and he cuts out pictures of vacuums from the ads. It's his scrapbook."

Julie won't argue with an estimate that their son's collection is worth "thousands," thanks to expenditures not only by Morgan's parents, but by Santa Claus, grandparents and others.

His personal collection of vacuums includes models by Electrolux, Dirt Devil, Kirby and Eureka. But it's Bissells with which he's most taken.

Ask him a vacuum's most important feature, and he answers, "The way it sucks." Mother Julie agrees, "It's really gotta suck."

Julie says their son has become something of a household name in Salem. It was a newspaper account there that tipped Bissell executives to his collection, and that notoriety is bound to grow.

In just the two hours following Morgan's visit Friday and its subsequent coverage by the Associated Press, Bissell phone lines were jammed by reporters from all over the United States and Canada.

TV and radio stations from Seattle to Washington, D.C., want in on the Morgan factor. And interest also has been expressed by The Tonight Show and Hard Copy.

Well before the limelight descended, though, Bissell execs were urging Morgan to choose some vacuum cleaners to take home – on the house, of course. One for your family, they said. And one for a favorite charity.

He spent an hour testing different models, finally settling on The Butler, a Power Partner, a Big Green Power Brush and a Bissell Plus.

He might put his freebies to the test. He might not. Morgan's mother, Julie, said her son is more absorbed with a vacuum's capacity for work than actually putting it to work.

When a reporter asked him what he would charge to vacuum the reporter's home, Morgan turned and grinned.

He said, "You couldn't afford it."

Just Like Mom:
Lots of Good in God's Kitchen

I can think of a lot of reasons why I shouldn't give money to God's Kitchen.

First off, I've been saving for a pool table.

Then there's the issue of those people the kitchen serves. Buncha freeloading moochers, if you want my opinion.

And let's face it – when real trouble surfaces, the affluent among us will pick up the pieces. After all, it's their destiny; they enjoy donning the garb of a goody-goody.

I would like to completely deny the last three paragraphs. But to lesser degrees, I have stooped to such rationale in the past, and I wonder if you have, too.

In our most honest moments, we have to admit that dismissing God's Kitchen as just another charity is the sentiment of someone with a hole in his heart.

And a full stomach.

But I'm not here to preach.

I'm here to beg.

With small exception, I tend not to solicit in this space. But I visited the Kitchen recently and could have cried.

It wasn't on account of the interview I conducted with the Kitchen's manager, who revealed that her operation is more than $50,000 in need.

Frankly, discussing dollars doesn't move me terribly. Same goes for hearing Carol Greenburg say that although she does sleep at night, it's only after long moments of prayer during which she wonders where the next cash donation will come from.

And it wasn't to learn that the Kitchen serves some 600 people a day through a trio of programs headquartered there – Meals On Wheels included.

Nor was I startled when Carol shared that every manner of expense is on the rise: for operations, utilities, fuel, for food.

Even when she said that, "This is the first year we've ever been in this position," I didn't come apart.

Hardly fazed me, frankly, when she explained how God's Kitchen is one of the few charities in our midst that never questions or demands anything of its recipients. "No questions asked," is how she put it.

I nearly came apart, though, a few days later, when unbeknownst to Carol and her staff, I slipped through the doors to watch the freeloaders, the moochers, the tableside panhandlers.

Because my wife and kids showed up.

So did the neighbor from around the corner.

You and your brother.

Somebody's grandfather.

They were all there, spooning soup from bowls – the only meal of the day for some.

Etched in their faces was more than the pain of hunger. It was the mirror image of God, and in each set of eyes, I saw reflected – for perhaps the first time – myself and the ones I love.

I talked to Carol Greenburg the better part of a month ago. But I purposely decided to wait until today to write this.

Mother's Day.

For 30 years, God's Kitchen has put on its apron, and just like your own mother, never wondered whether you deserved to eat today.

Thirty years. No questions asked.

And yet how many times have we wrapped our arms around this maternal figure and said, "Thanks?"

Instead, we have treated her perhaps like we've treated our own mothers: Taking her too much for granted.

We don't mean to. But sometimes, those who nurture and love us best are the last to be appreciated.

There are annual benefits to help God's Kitchen stay afloat – keep mother in the kitchen, if you will – feeding mouths who come and go and struggle their best to change, mend, ascend.

But right now, the Kitchen needs $52,000, and it needs it by July 1.

Carol can't say enough about the 2,500 volunteers who help the Kitchen go. And she gets tears in her own eyes to describe how, for the most part, "This place operates on the little guy sending a check.

"We open the mail, and that's how it comes in. We just hope."

That's no way to treat your mother. And a place that calls itself "God's Kitchen" shouldn't have to spend even one day in fear of not being able to provide.

Billiards can wait. My check's in the mail.

On Mother's Day, who's with me?

You can contribute to God's Kitchen at 303 S. Division Ave., Grand Rapids, MI 49503.

A Life of Limits, But Also Love

Stephen Patrick Jones never walked, much less ran or danced or played a game of baseball.

Hardly ever uttered an intelligible word.

His last days were relegated to a tiny upstairs bedroom at the corner of Neland Avenue and Sherman Street SE, where he spent time watching TV and waving and nodding to his nephew's and niece's friends, who called him "Uncle Patrick."

"Just tired," was how his sister and final caregiver, Leah Macklin, describes a brother who chose to slip away at 35 with as little fanfare as the world doled him out in life.

"There will be no funeral services," is the passage in his obituary that stopped me. When I asked Leah the reason, she said Stephen made the decision.

She could have financed it, she said, but her brother had wanted to simply leave this Earth in peace. "My brother had been through enough."

After he died March 4, they pinned his photo – the same one you see below – to a bulletin board at Lincoln School, a special place for special kids. Stephen had been a student there during the 1980s and '90s.

"Just a happy kid," recalled Leisa Barnes, a teacher there for 23 years. "He couldn't speak, but he had his way of communicating. If he was happy, he'd smile. If he was frustrated, you'd see a frown, or he'd shake his head.

"I lost contact. But I liked him a lot. He was my boy."

I look at the same picture, a bright-eyed youngster of 15, and wonder why more of us couldn't have had the privilege of saying that. That he was my boy, or my friend, or the kid down the block who loved to play in the rain, who announced himself with a whistle.

Too few of us called him anything, knew him in any capacity, realized he even existed.

Stephen Patrick Jones was a rare creation bound to play out his days in relative anonymity.

Crippled with cerebral palsy and other disabilities, he was unable to walk or talk. Doctors told his mother he wouldn't see age 2. His society was comprised of little circles – a class setting at school, a bus to and from, a bedroom in his home.

Not that he wasn't loved. A brother, Brian Macklin, took him into his own place after Stephen's mother died. When Brian died from complications of kidney and heart disease in the summer of 2005, Leah took over.

The family could have opted for institutionalization, but then who would bake him a cake on his birthday every Dec. 31?

Who would make sure he didn't miss his favorite TV shows – Springer and "Divorce Court" and "The Simpsons?"

Who would tuck him in at night, even as he was moving through his 20s and 30s, and whisper "I love you" at the close of day?

Watching him struggle to live could be tough, although Leah, 39, emphasized it was never a burden. "He was my brother."

Each day was a lot of the same – awakened around 7 a.m. to be bathed and fed and medicated, then a generous serving of television.

"I used to ask him if he wanted to go outside, but he'd shake his head no," says Leah. "I told him I could set him up in the driveway, but he didn't care for the outside."

In his youth, Stephen loved scrambled eggs and applesauce. Later, because of difficulty swallowing, he was fitted with a tube that delivered nutrients directly to his stomach.

In the end, he had trouble swallowing even his own saliva. Though a tracheotomy might have extended his life, he waved it off when his sister asked him to shake his head yes or no.

Tears stream down Leah's face to remember her last time with Patrick in the hospital, less than two weeks ago. "I told him that I loved him, and that I'd see him later."

They called her at 6 a.m. the Sunday before last to say he was gone. Respecting his wishes, Leah had her brother's remains cremated.

Most of us will never realize how far the ripples that were Stephen's life will spread. Maybe it's enough to know that in Leah's words, "He was here for a reason," to love and be loved.

"I think he's able to walk and talk now," Leah says of Patrick. "I think he's able to communicate with my mother and our brothers. I think they're all together.

"I think," she said of a kid who mattered, "that he's happy."

Obituaries Should Tell How One Lived

Most of us, myself included, never met or got to know Ruth E. Helderman.

But thanks to the obituary that ran last month in this newspaper, I have at least a few snapshots of her life. I know more about her than simply the day on which she died and how many survivors she leaves behind.

"Ruth," the notice read, "will be remembered by everyone who knew her for her exceptional wit, her love of music, her exuberant personality" – and this is the part that really interests me – "and truly remarkable black raspberry pie."

I would not have even come across Mrs. Helderman's obituary had it not been pointed out to me by Charley Moore, who recently retired as a newsman at The Press after 50 years.

Obits like Mrs. Helderman's, wrote Charley, "read so that I almost wish I had known them; they'd have been such fun and rewarding to be friends with."

I'm not yet a regular reader of The Press's obit section. But I've perused enough to know that most follow a formula.

Our own family adhered to it after my father died. Name, date of death, place of work, who was left to mourn....

Now, how I wish I'd included in his final notice that he had two holes in one on the same golf hole. How close he had come to playing professional baseball. That at wedding receptions, he had led a line of dancers while being pushed atop a food serving cart. The devotion he had showed to his family.

On the date Mrs. Helderman's obituary ran, 20 others joined her on the same page. But only two of those featured unorthodox windows into their lives.

Dennis Oberlin, for instance, officiated two high school state championship basketball games. He also taught driver education for 27 years. That SAYS something about a person.

Three columns over, I read that Juanita Zufelt "was a very independent, take-charge type of person with a huge heart." She also "arrived at her job at General Motors Plant #2 at least an hour early for 30 years."

Every day for 30 years – at least an hour early for work.

Wow.

After reading this page of obituaries that Charley Moore had mailed me with his letter, I called Reyers North Valley Chapel in Grand Rapids and talked to funeral director Tiffani Morrell.

Morrell had arranged for Mrs. Helderman's obituary to be published, and she remembered how the woman's two sons, Stephen and Thomas, took great care to make the notice personal.

Tiffani noted that obits can vary from region to region. In southern Illinois, for instance, from which she hails, the exact time of death is usually recorded in published death notices.

She acknowledges that a lot of families choose the formula that often appears in The Press – a fairly perfunctory run-down of facts.

Some families go a step further, however, and "want to let the world know how special this person was to them," Morrell said.

I couldn't agree more. Even at the risk of promoting sappiness, I'd enjoy reading about a guy's lifelong collection of fishing lures ... a mother's favorite bedtime story ... how so-and-so would be remembered by some for his wicked backhand.

A paid obituary is usually a family's last chance – sometimes their only chance – to trumpet a person's contributions.

And though the deceased may have traveled in small circles while alive, an obituary potentially introduces them to tens of thousands in the wake of their passing.

I say we share more than the five Ws.

Who preceded them in death. To which church they belonged. What to do in lieu of flowers.

Tell us what they did for a living, surely.

But tell us, too, how they lived, and whether fewer black raspberry pies in our midst is another reason to grieve.

How Cool: Clothes Drying in Breeze

This crazy autumn weather has brought a lot of positives.

More golf.

Less frost.

Better apples.

But of all the creature comforts that an extended summer brings, some of us appreciate one subtle gift as much as all the others.

Clothes on the line.

It is nothing less than ecstasy to crawl between sheets that have snapped and unraveled in a sun at this equinox and fall asleep on a pillowcase caressed all day by wind.

If you don't know the feeling, you've grown too accustomed to your Maytag dryer.

Not that you are alone. The once-ubiquitous clothesline is now the bane of upscale housing developments nationwide, even banned in some places.

Not a month ago, in fact, Susan Taylor, of Oregon, was featured on the front page of The Wall Street Journal for daring to take on her home association, which bans outdoor clotheslines.

"This bombards the senses," the newspaper quoted one of Taylor's neighbors as saying. "It can't possibly increase property values and make people think this is a nice neighborhood."

Paul and Anne Klein live in a very nice neighborhood, and it is altogether more picturesque for the clotheslines that bob in breezes there along 10 Mile Road NW in Sparta Township.

I was on my way to somewhere else this past weekend when I spied Paul's T-shirts and blue jeans soaking up a dose of noontime sun.

"If you drive through our area, which is a lot of farms," said Anne, "you'll see the same thing up and down the road – lots of T-shirts and lots of blue jeans."

Paul and Anne milk 40 cows on 104 acres, and by Saturday, given the chores associated with that operation, there are typically six loads of wash to do. In many ways, they enjoy life in an old-fashioned way. They heat their home with wood and they don't have an answering machine.

And 12 months a year, Anne eschews the dryer in favor of a rope. Wintertime? No problem, when you have the right kind of lines rigged in the basement.

Anne wouldn't have it any other way. "I can remember growing up on Page Street on the north end of Grand Rapids and I can't remember my mother not having a clothesline in our yard," she said. "It was a permanent fixture."

There is a system to Anne's line.

She hangs good shirts by the yoke, so as to disguise the presence of clothespins. She also hangs all shirts together, same for pants, and so on. Sometimes, she arranges things by color.

As for underwear, that gets hung nearest to the home, farthest from street view.

"So there's eye appeal," she said. "I know it sounds crazy, but you just do that."

She thinks it's "ridiculous" that some neighborhood covenants prohibit clotheslines – or more accurately, that anyone would prefer to live with such restrictions.

"You can't fix your car, either," she said of association rules against working on an auto in view of your neighbors. "And where to put your (satellite) dish."

For Anne, who works as a nurse at Spectrum Health, hanging laundry outdoors is one small way for her to express herself.

"We were talking about that just the other day," she told me. "So much of our days, we're just so busy. We don't have the opportunity to be creative.

"So we're creative in little things."

The Lost Reality of Alzheimer's

It's not every day that while driving your kids to school, you pass an old woman who looks as though she's lost – and in a most certain way.

For me, that day was Tuesday, and the short episode that ensued both gladdened and saddened.

I was taking two of our three boys to school, and I had a full boat when you factor in the puppy riding along.

In the middle of a hill on a busy street, I noticed a woman with white hair barely shuffling, and in what looked to be black winter boots.

She was wrapped in a red checkered blanket that only helped to make her look more out of place.

Because we were near the school, I decided to drop off the boys, then return to see what she might need.

When I reached her, she had not made much headway. I pulled over and asked if she needed help.

She seemed to sense the meaning of the question, but not how to answer it. She looked up and down the hill, and opened her mouth as if to say something, but the words fell out haphazardly.

"I ... don't remember."

"What I ..."

"If there ..."

I asked her if I could take her somewhere, and I thought she said, "the school."

My short exchange with her wasn't getting us anywhere, so I asked if she wanted a ride.

I finally managed to get her in my vehicle, and immediately was struck by a flashback from nearly 40 years ago.

Having grown up on Grand Rapids' West Side, my father would hustle us kids into the car for school and head down the alley behind our home to Sibley Street NW, which funneled to Lake Michigan Drive, long before the Ford Freeway was built.

On rare occasions, we would encounter working women making their way on foot to a smattering of factory jobs that dotted the Lower West Side.

He always asked if they wanted a ride.

They sometimes did, and so I grew up with the understanding that you at least made the offer.

But as the old woman settled into the seat, I was struck by something else my father had conveyed: every chivalrous act carried with it a risk.

Although my dad was kind and generous, he also understood how, in today's crazy world, offering people a ride could haunt you. Unscrupulous passengers could invent any scenario they liked, and the outcome might be reduced in court to their word against yours.

But it was apparent nearly from the start that this woman was no conniver. Instead, she was coming undone.

And so my suspicion was replaced by imagining that this could have been my grandmother. That almost certainly, she was someone's.

That miles away or around the corner, it was likely a relative or caretaker either was growing frantic, or would discover a reason to do so, and soon.

We made something less than small talk as I returned to the school, but I did manage to learn her name.

I escorted her into the building amid hundreds of laughing, bubbling small-fry, some of whom stared to see an old woman dressed as though she had just left a campfire.

By that time, a police officer had been summoned by other motorists who had spotted the woman on the road, and he and I pressed gently for information.

At one point, I wondered if she had an ID bracelet of some sort on either wrist.

Sure enough, I rotated her left arm to find a message etched in silver.

"Alzheimer's," read the first word.

Her name was inscribed, too, with an address and phone number in Lakeview, nearly an hour's drive to the north.

Turns out, she was staying with relatives down the hill and around the corner from where I had discovered her.

She was returned safely. But as I made my way to work, I couldn't help but wonder.

First, I wonder why I didn't stop on my way up the hill, before shipping the boys to school. There's no good reason.

Second, I wonder how many people passed the woman and assumed someone else would stop or assist her.

Third, I wonder what those who called for help might have done had they not had cell phones.

And finally, I wonder how many men and women with Alzheimer's or dementia wander homes or halls without ID bracelets, because their caretakers think this couldn't happen to them.

Think again.

Alas, Keys Get Locked in Car

This is a scary time of year, and I'm not referring to Halloween masks or the mark-up on kid's Christmas gifts or how Aunt Eileen insists on bringing homemade cranberry sauce to Thanksgiving dinner and there's no cranberries in it and still it's somehow red.

No. I am referring to how during the holidays guys lock their keys in the car with the motor running.

This is a phenomenon first experienced by the Three Wise Men, who were forced to abandon their teal-green Blazer and instead hitchhike some 20 bazillion cubits to Bethlehem, where they found not only a babe in swaddling clothes, but a nice enough carpenter named Joseph who doubled as a locksmith.

I have worked hard at extending this time-honored tradition on a near-annual basis, thanks to a hunk of cerebral cortex which renders me, and I quote my wife here, "You big stupe."

But only once did I actually trap one of our sons inside.

During the other instances, I have been routinely rescued either by my wife, if she was in the area and with spare keys, or by some Joe driving a wrecker and wielding a Slim Jim.

Every time she either mutters the "stupe" word or I end up handing over $40 to a wrecker driver, I swear that my next move will be to invest in a one-dollar magnetic key case, and attach it to the underside of the van.

Which I always immediately forget to do.

For some reason that escapes me, I am always doing this during the holidays. I would like to excuse such behavior by pointing out that I'm too busy making homemade gifts for everyone to bother with where I leave my keys.

Except that I go to Big Lots just like you do.

What finally cured me of this pesky rite was locking son Patrick in the minivan several years ago, when he was 2 and still wearing swaddling clothes.

We were parked outside my parents' home in Grand Rapids, and our destination was St. Mary's Hospital, to pick up Patrick's older brother, who'd spent the previous two days and nights at Saint Mary's for an asthma attack. My wife was with the patient, and so were her keys.

I figured we were only about 2 or 3 million cubits away, so I took my time strapping Patrick in, and after doing so, started the van, but then realized I hadn't closed the rear hatch.

As I did just that, I heard the sickening sound of a 2-year-old flipping the power locks into the closed position.

I tried hand signals and of course, loud and sustained screaming, but nothing worked. He just kept pressing the locks into the same closed status.

It was cold out, so I'd flipped the heater onto full-blast. In no time, Patrick – bundled up like the Michelin Tire Man and straightjacketed into his child-restraint seat – was sweating like a prizefighter.

When his whimpers and fidgeting turned to screams and thrashing, I scanned the landscape for a Joe, a Joe, any ol' Joe. I would have settled for a Vinnie, a Cecil, a Dale even.

Nearly an hour passed, and for reasons I don't recall, I couldn't locate my wife at the hospital. The wrecker couldn't promise quick response, either, so I did what any wise man would do.

I called the fire department.

Within minutes, Patrick was out. To this day, he does not care for the front seat, and neighbor kids still talk about how the firefighters drove off using the phrase "What a stupe!" a lot.

I, meanwhile, drove directly to a hardware store and purchased more keys and a magnetic case and for penance, lay in the snow and mud in my dress clothes in an effort to attach the case to the van's underbelly.

I lay there a long time in the slush looking for the perfect spot, and eventually I slid my hand up over a strut or whatever – I have no idea what I'm talking about – and pulled something down.

It was dark by now, not that anyone cared whether Mr. Stupe take all night if it meant avoiding another call to the fire department, so I had to get up from under the car and examine under the streetlight what I'd dislodged.

It was a gift from the previous owner of the van.

It was a magnetic key case, and inside, two spares.

Wow! It's Fall,
Plus Pointless Exclamations

Autumn doesn't deserve the trickling down of lame adjectives like "nice" and "pretty" and "beautiful."

"Nice" is something you had expected to happen anyway. "Pretty" doesn't convey a single calculable thing. And "beautiful," aside from whatever it is you're describing being in the eye of the beholder, may work for a solid rope to left-center. Or the perfect marriage between mortise and tenon.

But hardly autumn.

This is not to advocate dissecting the season so that the sheer delight wrought by color is overshadowed by a need to know. Still, the clinical explanation of photosynthesis may better be left to botanists, along with those capable of wringing romance from the process.

When it comes to nature, many of us need to walk a tightrope between simple recognition and total comprehension. I used to think that I may enjoy stargazing more if were to know all the constellations' names. I may someday, but for now, it's still enough to make their casual acquaintance, bathing in humility just to gaze upward.

Same with fireworks, which elicit an expected barrage of "oohs" and "aaahs" from the usual assortment of craning necks.

Yet few of us explore the magnitude of what goes into making pyrotechnics.

Autumn demands more, though, if only better and deeper explanations – at least to ourselves – for the way it affects.

This weekend and next, thousands will slide into autos for the obligatory "color tour," only to sit fairly numbed as each new rise proffers new angles on the annual phantasmagoria.

Human nature will prompt most of us to exclaim, most dully, "Isn't that beautiful!" and "Wow; look over there!"

But how many of us will connect, and either say so aloud, or somehow sear into our souls or at least inscribe onto paper in what specific ways it moves us?

How many people on color tours will get out of their cars and, rather than admiring a beech from afar, caress its smooth silver bark? Maybe feel a longing?

When is the last time you put your eyes only on a square inch or two of a single leaf, fingered its veins, marveled at the leathery texture oak ones boast?

And in sensory ways that "pretty" and "beautiful" could never evoke, what does autumn signal of your future, or wrest from your past?

On the most splendid of autumn days, like the ones we're experiencing now, it gathers from me the slow-motion image of my father's left arm.

He has been gone nearly two years – just three days sick and then disappearing over some pretty hill – so this snapshot is important to me: The slightly freckled arm perched on the driver's side door, the sleeve bunched up in the same wind that makes his hairs like tiny strands of seagrass waving, all eight of us crowded in a Country Squire station wagon, saying "pretty" and "beautiful" and "When are we going home?"

I sure don't want to go home now. I want to keep driving – to church, to a golf course, a ball field – with his left arm at ease.

When autumn comes and no one's watching, I'd like to climb into the back seat and have him drive me once more up Fruit Ridge Avenue, then further north, into the rarified air of counties where there are no words to describe the color.

If I were a little older, I'd jump up front and help him steer so he could operate the Super 8 movie camera from his seat, squinting through the viewfinder to bring every image home to our living room.

This is one of the ways we may seek autumn, acknowledging all the bittersweet that surfaces when caramel-coated skies come calling.

Old boyfriends. Dogs that have passed on. The first time you sipped cider and not just remembering what it's like to lie beneath a canopy of trees but bending to do it again.

It's a colorful tour alright. The secret is in knowing how to truly travel.

Breakfast Brings Bonding

One of my fondest early memories is that of serving Sunday Mass, then accompanying my father to the Knife & Fork Restaurant at the base of the old Pantlind Hotel.

It's funny, though, how sometimes I fail to realize that I can hand down those same rituals – until I'm roused by a 6-year-old voice at my side asking, "Dad, can we go to Arnie's for breakfast?"

It was his day off from the grueling rigors of kindergarten, so in the next instant, we were ordering cinnamon French toast from the cheery waitress with strong calves, and creating a Super 8 movie of our own.

"Dad," he said, "did you know that the space where I lost my tooth is perfect for when you want to take my temperature?

"The thermometer fits right there," and he opened up a mouth full of syrup and battered bread to show me.

I'm not the best listener. It's easy for me to drift, folding in my own mental needs among those across the table from me.

But somehow, this morning was different. Maybe it was the lime-green wares finally being offered up by the deciduous trees outside our window.

But most likely, it was in recognizing a pure moment, unfettered by some pending deadline; a framed photo basking in spontaneity.

So I asked cheery if she had a spare pen, and I wrote as we ate.

We wandered and wondered around our separate worlds some, and I came to the conclusion that if I thought like an artist, like a romantic – like a kid – we really pedaled down a lot of the same byways.

"Dad," he ventured, "do you eat your favorite food last or first? Because if mom packs me two desserts for lunch, I have to figure out which one I like more, and then I always save that for last."

He was conveying the joys of delayed gratification. So I countered with, "It's like getting you that new baseball mitt. We could go right out and get it now or think about it for a few days and go later."

"Yup."

He made a monster of his napkin. I demonstrated how to play football with a piece of the place mat.

"I wonder what it would be like to be a fish," he said, "and swim around all day."

"What if you got caught by a fisherman?" I asked.

"I wouldn't eat the salmon," he informed me, and I knew he was talking about the female's eggs, used as bait.

He ate a little more and gazed up at me. "I think I got spring fever."

Those of you without kids might have turned to Sports by now. I can understand. At a hair shy of 45, I already sound like an old man ruminating.

Earlier this month, an astute Grandville High School senior named Libby Struik asked me a most poignant question while shadowing me at work: "Do you ever think your columns are too autobiographical?"

Maybe, I allowed. But not if I'm somehow connecting with common experience.

On second reflection, though, perhaps I'm trying to apologize for the way I somehow fail to wrap myself in my three boys' doings. We all fall down.

I can't remember specifics of what my own father and I talked about at the Knife & Fork. It was bacon and eggs and a newspaper, I'm sure, peppered with bits of conversation. Geography class. Whose birthday was next. McAuliffe's weird stance.

The important thing is connecting, which requires a conscious effort to involve.

It means growing older, but not necessarily up, so far up that you risk affirming your world as entirely separate from theirs.

I know a young girl who plays soccer. To my knowledge, her daddy has never been to a game.

I think they could both use some French toast.

Icon's First Pitch Dazzles Crowd

How do you improve on an already perfect game like baseball?

You bring in the say-hey kid from the neighborhood and let him toss out the ceremonial first pitch.

That's exactly what they do at Riverside Park, which Northern Little League calls home, and where lumbering David Schultheiss is the biggest fan.

David got the call a little after 9 a.m. Saturday, just like he did last year, and lobbed a perfect strike to the plate that helped kick off the season for a blue-collar ball league that's been around since at least 1960.

"Let's play ball!" David barked into the microphone to the thunderous applause of several hundred people who braved frigid conditions Saturday as a stiff breeze swept off the Grand River.

And then he gave his trademark greeting – two thumbs up and a crooked smile to melt bricks.

They could have invited the mayor to fire the first pitch, of course. Or a city commissioner or local business owner. Some pillar.

Instead, they chose everybody's buddy, a special person who works the Little League crowd like a seasoned politician, but with only this as his agenda: friendship.

"We first did this last year, and people had tears in their eyes," said Cheryl Johnson, 40, whose daughter and two sons play on Northern teams.

"I grew up down here, and David has been coming to this park every single night for years."

A thousand people will tell you the same story: how Dave makes his way from the home he keeps on Knapp Street NE to cheer on kids whose names he doesn't even know.

"He sat right there and watched our entire practice about four weeks ago," said Dean Marshall, who coaches a T-ball team sponsored by Coit Gravel. "I mean, the whole practice. And then he said he'd be back for the next one, and he was."

Added Joey Sutherlin, 37, as he shielded son Chase, 2, against the cold: "Every neighborhood kid knows Dave, from the time they're little. You can't go anywhere on the North Side – not Northfield Lanes, Briggs Pool or this park – that he's not there.

"Literally, he's an icon."

I first met David about 10 years ago and was so touched by his sense of compassion that I followed him around the better part of a day as he cut neighbors' lawns.

He spent as much time cooing at flitting sparrows as he did with the mower. "They're so darn cute," he said time and again of the birds. "Lookit that, lookit that; they're not hardly afraid. So cute. So cute."

Because Dave can resemble the character Lennie in Steinbeck's "Of Mice and Men," both in appearance and tone, it's important for newcomers to the North End to sometimes meet him via a third party, said Mike Helsel, Northern's president.

"Every year, we make sure to introduce him to new families who might be put off a bit by his exuberance," Helsel says. "We want everybody to feel comfortable with Dave."

Though 55, Dave generates all the innocence of a 10-year-old, giving high-fives to anyone who'll take them, and greeting people with hearty handshakes, earning him nicknames such as "Shakin' Dave" and "Howyadoin' Dave."

Until a couple of years ago, Dave lived with parents Fred and Faye. They've both since passed, and Dave tends the modest home with help from a nearby sister.

He's become an expert at using the bus to get around town, but his favorite haunt is just steps away at the park, where baseball games run virtually every afternoon and evening, seven months a year.

On Saturday, teams such as "Grand Rapids Auto Parts" and "Kay's Pharmacy" and "Kool Toyota" took to the fields and stood for opening ceremonies, which included the singing of the National Anthem by Aubrey Clark, 11.

Her great-grandfather, George LeMire, then asked God's blessing on the fields, and reminded everyone Our Lord's favorite sport is baseball – if you just re-work the opening to the Book of Genesis to sound like "In the big inning..."

Then it was Dave's turn, and after setting down a plastic bag filled with sandwiches and V-8 Juice to sustain him throughout another long day at the park, he gripped the ball and let it fly.

He raised his arms in glee. "That was a strike, wasn't it?" he asked no one in particular.

And who would argue?

Right down the middle.

On a Saturday at the ball field, something perfect.

Plates Filled By Generosity

"Sometimes I love Tom Rademacher, and sometimes I hate his articles," wrote Lucy and Ed, a couple from the West Side of Grand Rapids.

And with that, they signed their letter "Happy Mother's Day."

And tossed in a check for $200.

Lucy and Ed, I couldn't have put it more succinctly myself. Heck, even I hate the stuff I write sometimes.

But I'm sure glad I wrote what I did two Sundays ago, on Mother's Day, when I revealed the plight of God's Kitchen, a food broker for the needy among us.

Following that column, which detailed how God's Kitchen was in need of $52,000 by July 1, the "haves" among us responded to help the "have nots."

In last Tuesday's mail to the Kitchen at 303 S. Division Avenue, workers dumped out checks and cash totaling $16,000.

The next day, over $18,000 rolled in.

Then eight thousand ... and so on.

In a week's time, more than 425 people had dug deep to help, sending in checks for as little as $5 and as much as $5,000.

As of Monday, the total stood at $52,723, exceeding not only the goal, but the Kitchen's wildest expectations.

"This is more typical of what we receive in November and December, during the Christmas season," said an elated Carol Greenburg, the Kitchen's director.

"It is so humbling to get this kind of response. To imagine that kind of social responsibility ... it really and truly is a mark of Christian love, to give with no questions asked."

"It sure takes the pressure off," Greenburg said on behalf of the Kitchen, which this year celebrates three decades of sharing with the hungry.

I'd simply written on Mother's Day how God's Kitchen is a lot like a mother – that rarest of creatures capable of unconditional love.

But apparently, it hit a nerve. Here's what you wrote in letters that delivered generous donations:

"My husband used to contribute food," wrote one woman who sent $25. "But he isn't here anymore. So I will fill in for him. I wish I could send more."

"I read (the column) and decided to make a few sacrifices this month for God's Kitchen," Nancy wrote. "I hope this ($100) helps."

"After spending the afternoon with my family for Mother's Day, I came home and read the article ... regarding your work with God's Kitchen. I must admit

I felt a little guilty since we had an abundance of food to choose from and no one went home hungry." The unsigned note contained two twenties.

"I have read and re-read and also shared this article with others, each time crying harder than the last," Jane wrote.

"My mother – my best friend, – passed away three days after Christmas this past year. I want to remember her by giving to an organization that most closely reflects the image of Mom."

"(The column) made very clear that most of us do not realize what is happening in our city," Doris wrote. "I did not know that Meals on Wheels is a part of God's Kitchen. I hope this ($100) check will help."

"I've decided that I've been very blessed this year, and it's not even over," Sharon wrote. "A few of my neighbors eat at God's Kitchen, and except for His graces, I could be there, too."

Splitting Wood: A Spiritual Side

There are few things so disarming as a woodpile, poetry in 16-inch lengths stacked in what one could argue is both a scattering and perfect symmetry.

I know that not everyone feels this way. Three days ago, a friend faced the chunks I was splitting and when I hinted that this was more than just wood, she said, "I don't know what the big deal is, but my husband feels the same way."

He goes into their woodlot, she continued, and takes way too much time selecting just the right tree for sacrifice, one that will both heat their Vermont home and promote saplings struggling beneath its canopy, and lower still, growth of finer dimensions - lichens and fungi and their microscopic hosts.

I nodded. I know. If trees are to be treated as objects of respect, then their sum parts are no less sacrosanct. Into our hands they deliver dimensional pine, bowls of walnut, fine furniture from Birdseye maple, baseball bats of white ash.

And this pile before me, this pile of red oak will be for burning, a function borne of a bittersweet decision that began with musing over the eventual purchase of a wood stove, years back.

Sixteen trees were felled in all, topped first by professional cutters, and mostly in the name of safety. Six alone leaned too close to the house, and it was their proclivity to bend - not thunder and lightning - which kept me awake during storms.

So tree pieces stand here now, and waiting. One of the barebacked cutters had stared at the sheer volume here and shook his head.

"Lotta wood here," he said, working a plug of Kodiak from jaw to jaw. "You'd be surprised how many people leave it layin', say they're gonna split it up and don't."

Then, as if wondering what this latest client would do, he spit, and said it again: "They just leave it layin'."

It has been a week now since he and his two co-workers and their chainsaws and climbing spikes departed, leaving me with slabs of red oak for company.

I did a lot of looking at it at first, remembering how I'd split small amounts in the past but never more than a few hours' worth.

You need a good heavy maul and enough sense to keep your legs spread during the delivery. Wedges are a boon, but stubbornness is an apt stand-in.

My toil draws onlookers. "You can rent those log-splitters," says one neighbor.

"That's nice oak," offers another visitor, an old man who's worked with wood. "Not like elm," he says. "Oak's got good, straight grain. Elm'll wear you out, though."

I would rather talk of elm's quirks than engage in a conversation about log-splitters, so he and I talk.

He chuckles at my reluctance to acquire wedges, but he understands. We discuss grain and hardness and oak's adaptability.

I tell him I enjoy the explosion, the point at which an upright piece yields to the maul and there is a loud pop and then there are two airborne pieces and then only the sound of my heart beating in my ears.

I tell him I will never tire of that, of that moment. He nods. He asks, "What will you do when you're done?" I surmise that he knows the answer is a painful one, that there will only be the stacking to do, and then a vacuum where labor reigned.

Every piece is unique, painted with a different shade of orange, and striated in ways no canvas could ever capture.

Often, I bend to smell it. It doesn't remind me of anything, but it is a rich, pungent scent, and worth doing over and over.

It is hot, and I am drinking cold well water and burning calories. I do this six consecutive evenings before I look around to see that I am finished, and as I had suspected, it is as much a forlorn feeling as one of satisfaction.

My friends lay in a great pile, big as a car. My back and shoulders ache, prompting a comment from within that I have not been able to express for too long a time, but really, it is a good kind of hurt.

Dishes and Drains and Life at Dusk

There never seemed to him anything profound about vacuuming the drapes or scrubbing the kitchen floor or taking out trash.

So there was nothing stirring in him when he went – reluctantly – into the basement to clean out the sewer drain.

He had a partner for errands around the house now, but they had bargained how if he would do the "boy" stuff, she would do the "girl" stuff. (They still believed in gender stereotypes – if only for the sake of convenience – and were not ashamed to admit it.)

Spitting and cussing about how filthy the snake line was, and wishing he'd cleaned it the last time he'd used it to attack the beast, he knelt to do battle with the hole in the floor.

I hate doing this, he thought. We should buy a different home just because of this. Who cares about the leaded glass and the woodwork that's never been painted when the drain clogs…?

Snake in one hand and handle in the other, he clumsily worked the rusted tool, listening to the garbled sound of metal against drain tile.

He was only hoping to get finished with the task and on to another when she came running down the basement steps. She rarely ran unless she was outdoors. She did it best galloping along a beach, exactly at dusk, after the sun slipped away, leaving only candlelight.

But she was running down the basement steps, and before he could turn to her, snake in hand, she was telling him how it had moved.

It had moved.

Not like a bird in the palm of a hand, as one had told her it might be. And it was not a quickening, either, as another had predicted.

No, it was stronger than that – three significant kicks, and it had happened not as she and the husband were together on a couch, or tucked away in bed, but instead while she was doing dishes by hand and he was at their sewer drain.

He let go the snake, forgetting about the clog, and the leaded glass and woodwork that never had been painted. He hugged her hard, forgetting how dirty he was, thinking only of the movement.

Against the backdrop of dank and crumbling basement walls and a drain that called to be fixed, he thought in three-quarter time: Kick, kick, kick. One, two, three. It had moved.

I am here.

His mind was still waltzing when she had the husband put his hand on her belly, and he was trembling when he did, so he didn't know if it was another kick or his own pulse he felt.

There was celebrating in the basement, brief but profound and entirely unexpected. It was the first time they remembered ever celebrating anything in the basement.

The husband eventually went back to the drain, clinking the snake in and out and around and around, trying for some resolve. Between efforts, he would pause, and in his mind's eye, a child of 3 or 4 in underwear with "I Love Grandma" stamped on the butt would run pell-mell down a beach.

When he finished in the basement, he put away the snake, and never bothered to clean it. And when he went upstairs and outside to breathe the outdoors, it was dusk. It was exactly dusk.

CHAPTER 2

Lilt

Dog Collar Delivers Bite

The invisible fencing device can put its owner on all fours when put to the test. The shocking truth?

Those electronic dog collars work.

I know. I put one to the test last week, and not on my dog's neck, but my own.

In fact, if I were a dog right now and still wearing the little zapper-contraption, I wouldn't be typing this. I'd be on all fours confined to the yard.

And liking it.

Boy, would I ever.

My little experiment began germinating a few years ago, after noticing a golden retriever near where we who live barked at passersby but never left the yard.

The secret? A transmitter in the home or garage sends a radio signal through an antenna wire buried in Rover's yard. The wire then sends a signal to a tiny receiver worn on the dog's collar. The signal uses a combination of beeps – and shocks – to help Old Shep learn his boundaries.

The system was introduced some 20 years ago by the Invisible Fence Co. Inc. though copycat models have surfaced since the original patents expired.

Our do-it-yourself neighbors, Kim and Becky Naessens, installed a system themselves for their black lab, Cosmo, and dang if it doesn't work. Best of all, they've got no ugly fences or dog runs or dangerous system of ropes and chains.

But in my mind, this question has always persisted: What's it feel like?

Now I've got as much respect for volts and amperage as the next guy. And I've screwed up enough times while doing electrical work to know what a real shockeroo feels like. Sort of like being stung by a bee on steroids.

But a doggie collar? That's new territory. And I figure a columnist's gotta do what a columnist's gotta do. So I drove to see Barb Hopper, office manager for Invisible Fence in this area.

She touted her system, of course. Raved about it, actually. And why not? Invisible Fence and its cousins aren't just for dogs anymore. They're being used to control damage from deer to fruit and other cash crops. Old McDonald just buries a line around his acreage and fits a few dogs with collars. The dogs chase the whitetails off the plantation but no further.

Hopper emphasized that a pet owner provide visual and audio cues before actually exposing the dog to shocks; it's part of the training Invisible Fence provides.

In any case, Hopper said other dog owners – including skeptics – have asked to feel the poke delivered through the prongs, but only via their fingers, and for just a split-second. So at my request, she hooked up a mock system and let me have at it.

"YOW!" I said, jumping back. "That hurts!"

"It is unpleasant," she replied. "But it doesn't hurt nearly so much as getting hit by a car or a truck, or undergoing major surgery at the vet."

Hopper surprised me by saying that even this much juice "isn't enough for some dogs."

Aggressive breeds can possess a higher than normal threshold of pain. The owners of such animals, who represent less than 2 percent of customers, get their money back, then consider other options.

Me? I needed to know what sort of breed I was.

"What if I wanted to try the probe around my neck?" I asked Hopper. She shook her head. "We wouldn't allow that."

But my friends Kim and Becky – at least I think they're my friends – would.

"Go for it," said Kim, who confessed that he, too, had long flirted with the idea of self-inflicted shocks. A regular guy.

For starters, I pressed Cosmo's probe to my shirt-covered belly, then walked through the "field" as it's called, in this case, about six feet wide. Nothing.

Had my shirt gotten in the way? Yup.

I pressed the probe to my bare arm and tried again.

"Yow-EE!" I screamed.

But I wouldn't be satisfied until the fiendish collar was about my neck. Readers, I kept telling myself, deserved nothing less.

Knowing enough to keep the probes away from the carotid arteries that carry blood to my brain (such as it is), I arranged the collar so the probes would deliver their bite to the back of my neck.

Then through the field I went, at a mild trot. Very dog-like, I thought to myself.

Well let me tell you. I felt that bolt all the way down my back. I twitched. I spasmed. I jerked. I writhed. By the time I'd gotten through the field, I'd emitted a primordial scream that Becky would later define as "unspellable."

"Actually," she said, "it reminded me of a bad death scene in a B movie."

When it was over, I found myself knocked to both knees, glad to be free of the field.

Glad to have it done with.

Glad I'm not a dog.

Home Alone: It's So Scary

"Homines libenter id quod volunt credunt."

Ol' Caesar sure had it right when he uttered these words in Latin more than, well, I suppose it had to be at least 300 or 400 years ago.

Translated, it means "Men easily believe what they want to," and it's an apt description of my own confidence level the morning my wife and oldest son left earlier this month for a week-long historical tour of the East Coast, which, if I'm not mistaken, included the birthplace of Julius the Very Quotable himself.

But let's digress from my knowledge of all things both historical and geographical, and focus for a moment on my abilities in the area of homemaking. This will be short.

I know men who are able to keep house. I am not one of them. To wit:

– When you run out of dish-washing detergent, something called "Murphy's Oil Soap" will not serve as a substitute, unless you enjoy the taste and feel of bubbly lacquer with your next meal.

– It's best to retrieve clothes from a washing machine sooner than 48 hours after you've finished the load. Similarly, clothes left more than a day or two in the dryer will have people in town whispering about the shirts and shorts your kids wear in public. (Thanks, by the way, to everyone who dropped clothing off on our front stoop, but we really are doing fine now.)

– Don't believe those clips from movies in which Mr. Mom Wannabees spot-dry clothing in a microwave oven. It doesn't work, and let's not even touch on the aromas it produces in what used to be our eating area.

– Dogs CAN survive without water for three consecutive days. (Just kidding).

– Changing one's underwear daily isn't absolutely necessary, especially if the only places you're visiting are yard sales and roadside stands.

Not that my wife was aware of any of the above while she was gone.

Aside from knowing a little Latin, I am also smart enough to understand that when she called each evening, my job was to keep her confidence level high regarding the home front. So a typical conversation might go like this:

"Hi Tom, how's everything?"

"Just super, honey. Incidentally, how sick would a kid have to be before you consider having his stomach pumped?"

Then I might say, "Ha-ha, just kidding," and let her know that it only turned out to be a mild case of food poisoning, and geesh, I guess it's really true what they say about not using the same dish you made raw hamburger patties on to actually serve the finished product.

Of course, there are some advantages to living a quasi-bachelor life while your spouse is out of town. For one, you can eat all the garlic you want and breathe in any direction after getting into bed.

At least the dog never complained.

Champ Nails Another Victory

For a living, Cheryl Fisher drives a truck.

For kicks, she drives nails.

The 37-year-old West Sider is so good at it, in fact, that for the second consecutive year, she was crowned the National Naildriving Champion for women in an annual contest sponsored by Stanley tools.

You may have seen a photo of her with arm raised in triumph, and read of her exploits in a Press article earlier this week.

On behalf of swaggering men everywhere, I wanted a chance to pit my own hammering skills against hers, in nailhead to nailhead competition.

I rolled up to the Seventh Street NW address that Cheryl had provided. It didn't exactly lend itself to the home of a national champion of anything. It's a modest two-unit apartment building with a front porch that has seen better days.

I approached the front door and Cheryl was there to greet me with a very firm handshake. Strong, I thought. But I've slammed home a few nails myself over the years. She'll be crying in her tool belt by the time we're through.

Once inside, we reviewed her accomplishment. She'd flown last week to Dallas with her parents, two older sisters and a handful of nieces and nephews, all of whom had accompanied her to watch her defend the title at the International Builders' Show.

The first year, Cheryl had done it on a lark. She was in Dallas to take in the same show, and saw an ad for the nailing competition. It enticed with $750 in first-prize money.

What the heck, she figured, and went on to win the competition.

This year, she nearly didn't qualify, despite practicing nearly every night throughout December by hammering nails into boards out on the front porch.

To make it into the finals, you have to be fastest on one of three qualifying days to drive four nails into a 6-by-6-inch block of treated Southern Yellow Pine.

In the first two days, she'd failed. But on Sunday, she rammed home four nails – 16-penny variety each measuring 31/2 inches long – in just 2.43 seconds. It was a record for women.

Sunday evening at the finals, where contestants must pound in three nails instead of four, she beat all comers to reign again and rake in another $750, plus assorted goodies.

For 10 years, Cheryl has been loading lumber and driving a flatbed truck for Hager Distribution Inc. of Wyoming. So she doesn't have especially pretty hands. Just pretty strong ones.

A native of the Clare County town of Farwell, Cheryl earned a degree in criminal justice from Ferris State University before moving to Grand Rapids 12 years ago. In her lifetime, she has built garages and sheds alongside her father, a licensed contractor. Her mother directs the Home Builders' Association of Central Michigan.

As we walked outside to confront a few dozen preset nails, I wandered back to my own building experience. A shed or two. A cottage. And more shingling than I wanted to remember. I even hold a builder's license. Frankly, I was already feeling sorry for the kid.

Cheryl had imbedded some 16-penny nails into a 6-by-6. She explained how, in competitions, a special template ensures that every nail is set to the same depth – and distance from one another. "This is pretty close," she said, handing me a stopwatch and reaching for a Stanley 20-ounce hammer.

She went first, resting her hammer on the block and telling me to announce the start with "Ready, set, GO!" She looked a little sloppy in burying three nails with a time of nearly 10 seconds.

"Try again," I said, trying not to sound too patronizing.

"Whamwhamwhamwhamwham!"

I gulped. She'd found her tempo, ramming the threesome home with seven or eight strokes, and in less than 5 seconds.

She handed me the Stanley. It felt heavy, awkward. I had the sudden urge to bake some cookies.

Whack! My first nail bent over like a licorice twist. Quickly, I righted it with the claw end of the hammer. Wham! Whack! I was hitting more wood than nail. I finished with a dismal 10.5.

"Try again," Cheryl said.

"Whackshrt! I bent the first nail. Righted it. Then – phrriing! – I bent the second. I was approaching a half minute when Cheryl suggested I begin anew.

On my third try, I registered a time of 7.8 seconds.

"The men's record for three," said Cheryl, "is 1.09 seconds. If a guy doesn't drive home three nails with three blows, he doesn't stand a chance."

Is my apron showing?

Could You Pass July 4 Exam?

Many younger people are foggy on the details – or downright clueless – when it comes to Independence Day and its place in history.

Last week, I was intrigued by a radio broadcast that chastised Americans for not knowing enough of their own country's history.

Specifically, they were targeting the events surrounding July 4, 1776, and how we not only take our freedom for granted, but sorely lack an understanding of how we came to acquire it.

Nonsense, I thought, and the next day found myself quizzing our fifth-grader-to-be.

"What do we celebrate on the Fourth of July?" I asked.

He appeared stumped.

"You know," I coached, "Independence Day."

A knowing look suddenly crossed his face. "Oh yeah," he said. "That's when Will Smith killed all the aliens."

"Noooooo."

"Oh wait," he countered. "Doesn't it have something to do with the Germans?"

Ouch.

Two days later, I fanned out in my quest for more knowledgeable Americans, visiting a large shopping mall to interview folks in our midst.

In all, I talked with 28 people, purposely focusing mostly on men and women in their late teens and early 20s. After all, I reasoned, they'd be the ones fresh out of high school and college history classes.

In exchange for their answers, I agreed in large part to use respondents' first names only.

In each case, I asked, "Why do we celebrate the Fourth of July?"

Of 28, only nine answered straightaway that it was a celebration of Independence Day, or that it was the anniversary of the signing of the Declaration of Independence.

Here's how the rest fared ...

I found 20-year-old Nicole first. "Why do we celebrate the Fourth of July?" I asked her.

She looked puzzled. "Was it a war or somethin?'"

Josh, 17, turned beet red, and answered, "I feel so stupid; I should know this.

Kelly, 20, answered "Oh my gosh. I'm too young." Then she added, "I learned it somewhere."

Tammy, 34, told me the Fourth of July commemorated "When our country became our country."

Her 13-year-old son only knew that "It's when we watch fireworks, go to Sand Lake, and shoot hoops."

Thalia, whose age I forgot to ask (she looked 20-something) fielded my question and said, "Am I allowed to make a phone call?"

Myia, age 19, said, "Didn't they sign something?"

Jeremy, age 15, knew that we celebrated "Independence Day" on July 4, but then added, "Isn't that the day we won the Civil War?"

His mother, standing beside him, wasn't sure.

When I posed the question to friends Kacy, 20, and Sue, 21, Kacy turned to Sue and pleaded for her to answer: "You're in school; I'm not," she said. She then turned to me and giggled. "I'm not very good in history."

Sarah, Jillian, and Kelley, all in their 20s, stood for my question next. After Jillian answered correctly, I challenged the other two. "Did you know?" I asked.

"Now that she says it, I do," said Kelley, "but I wouldn't have been able to do it myself."

Still talking with the same three, I asked, "Do you know who authored the Declaration of Independence?"

Before the other two could answer, Sarah pumped her fist high into the air.

"That I know," she boasted, and yelled out "Francis Scott Key!"

"That's close," I said glumly, and heard neither friend correct her.

The last person I interviewed was Gin Clausen. She is 50. Not only did she know about the Declaration of Independence, but that in the days leading up to its signing, the Continental Congress was meeting mostly in Philadelphia's Carpenter's Hall, since it was one of the few institutions not controlled by the British.

Gin Clausen, by the way, was born in Canada.

She has been an American citizen for six months.

Holiday Sweaters Leave Me Cold

Allow me to introduce you to my holiday sweater:

It's red.

Now, allow me to introduce you to my wife's holiday sweater:

It's red and green and white with Frosty dancing in a city of gingerbread and reindeer dashing across a sky of jingle bells and sugarplum fairies and sprigs of mistletoe and big bushy wreaths and Hans Brinker's skates and flaming candles and flakes of snow falling everywhere.

And that's just on her left arm.

OK, I'm exaggerating.

Still, you can broadcast Burl Ives at Thanksgiving and roll out the Yule log in September or even try to entice me into buying a Tickle Me Elmo in June.

But nothing says "The Holidays" like a woman's sweater gobbed up with kitschy Christmastime cues.

Remember when you were in kindergarten and Mrs. Constantino gave you a jar of mucilage and a handful of macaroni and some yarn and sequins and pine cones?

There's your holiday sweater!

I came into the kitchen the other morning to find Hollie The Lovely wearing a pullover that – let me try to convey this subtly – didn't exactly look like something Scarlett Johansson would wear to a photo shoot.

It had to weigh more than a cord of wood, given the flotilla of bric-a-brac and other three-dimensional wintertime stuff affixed to every square inch.

"Are those real cookies on your shoulders?" I asked, reaching.

"NO!"

My friend Jim – he's gender-sensitive – wonders whether the holiday sweater is to women what a set of Carhartt bib overalls are to men.

Maybe. Except Carhartts actually serve a purpose. And nobody mistakes you for a scarecrow.

A holiday sweater, on the other hand?

Well, if you were to slice it up just right, it would make a dandy apron for the Christmas tree.

"I like my sweater," my wife insisted.

But any guy realizes that's merely pig-Latin for: "You know Aunt Untrendy bought me this, and if I don't wear it, she'll be hurt."

Never mind that Aunt Untrendy has been gone a decade now, pronounced dead of suffocating beneath a turtleneck laden with 10 lords-a-leaping fashioned from cast iron pipe cleaners.

Not that I deserve a soapbox from which to deliver a speech on fashion faux pas. The last pair of pants I bought were designed to offer camouflage while hunting in the snow. I own exactly one suit. And I believe that orange and blue look good together.

But wearing one of those extra-busy holiday sweaters only confuses guys, in that we just don't know where and how to look.

For example, let's say you've got a scene from Whoville roaming your frontside. Everyone knows that Man Rule No. 14 limits to 1.2 seconds the amount of time we can openly scan your sweaterage.

Therein lies the problem. We want to offer a friendly compliment. But spend too much time checking out your Currier & Ives, and there's a burly boyfriend ready to make us play Bob-for-Breath in the eggnog bowl.

It's a shame, really, that more women don't choose neckwear to make a holiday statement.

Take those battery operated ties, for instance, that light up Santa's nose when you pull the little string.

Now those are cool.

Taking Your Children to School? Stop and Drop

Today's kids aren't fat and lazy because they eat badly and watch too much TV.

Today's kids are fat and lazy because nincompoop parents who drive those kids to school insist on dropping them off directly at the front door, creating not only roly-poly children but also perfect examples of how to grow up and become a butthead.

And you know who you are: Every morning, after laying out clothes and making a lunch for Precious, you buckle him or her into a pre-heated car, drive to school, and then engage in behavior so boorish and double-dang rude that perhaps you need to be schooled.

I'm not bashing kids with special needs. Nor moms and dads who motor their young ones to school by the rules. Just those who think the driveway and parking lot were created for them and them alone.

You crawl. You cavort. You cave in to bad etiquette.

Here's a big fat hint: You're not the only person in the world racing against an 8 o'clock school bell. There are others called "teachers" trying to get there, too – not to mention principals, janitors, support staff, vendors and OK, that one guy in every district who wears a funny hat, shows up at all the sporting events, and everyone knows by just one name. Like Dale. Or Watson. Or Bubba.

Which means you have no right to be the following person:

– The dad who, because he feels he's "All That," doesn't release the kid from the car until he's absolutely in front of the flagpole. To toss the kid out any earlier – and help quicken the flow of traffic – would be a sign of weakness. (Note: These are the same dads who live their lives in the left lane of the highway, whether passing or not).

– The mom who, after being beside their kid for a 20-minute ride in, suddenly decides to have a long conversation with their student just as they pull curbside. Let me put this gently: "GET THE $*#(&* OUT OF THE CAR!!!"

– The parent who, after pulling up, has the audacity to exit the vehicle so they can help Lil' Johnny unload his junk. Hey Skeezix – why do you think everybody keeps calling your Johnny "Lil'?"

– The mommy who, after dropping off her kid, decides to hold up the entire line by yakking it up with other delinquent moms about how cold it is, whether Brawny is better than Bounty, and where she's shopping today.

The honking horns and looks of defeat and disgust and disdain belong to all the other parents behind you. I'm talking about conscientious parents who push their kids out of their cars at the first safe opportunity.

Parents who know the difference between "love" and "enable."

Parents whose kids actually get some exercise, so that when they walk, their corduroy thighs don't "swish" against each other to announce that, "My mommy coddles me, my mommy coddles me...!"

Let's do our kids a favor – and in the process free up those clogged traffic routes, the parking lots, the emergency lanes.

Tonight, tell your kid that tomorrow morning, they're getting out of the car when you say, "I love you, now go," and not when they're square to the front door.

They'll squawk some, of course, mostly because it will force them to consider real footwear rather than the flip-flops or bedroom slippers they insist wearing in all four seasons.

Tell 'em that's tough.

Tell 'em you're just trying to teach them to do the right thing.

Tell 'em you can hear their thighs.

Dog Eyedrops Bring Backlash

My wife Hollie is hardly a dog, and yet she went to work the other day with a leash, collar and Milk Bone biscuits hidden in her lunch bag.

It was my little doing, of course, and not hers, as she is suffering enough just from the verbal abuse in the aftermath of what happened this past Monday morning.

She's a teacher, so maybe it was the shock of having to go back after a two-week Christmas break.

Or perhaps it's due to the weird weather we've been having, compliments of El Whatever-O.

Whatever the cause, something prompted her to pay too little attention to what sort of drops she was putting in her irritated right eye that morning.

Unless you keep house like Martha Stewart, let's face it, your medicine cabinet is probably a cornucopia of surprises. You've got pills that have expired and elixirs you no longer use and maybe even a vial or two of unmarked solutions.

The morning Hollie reached for eye relief, she had four options: HypoTears, OcuClear, Visine Extra and Atropine Sulfate.

Even now, nearly a workweek later, she can't explain why she opted for the fourth, or even whether she'd spotted the other three on the cabinet shelves.

A part of her, she would later say, figured that Atropine Sulfate is what I was given a while back to help treat the removal of a wood splinter from my eye.

But it wasn't. I was given something altogether different, along with a stern warning to wear safety glasses next time I operate any power saw, in this case, a 12-amp Makita 10-inch Model LS1020 miter saw capable of 4,100 rpms-arg-arg-arg.

But enough about my own ineptness.

Immediately after tipping her head back to receive two or three drops of this Atropine Sulfate, her right pupil dilated. Her vision blurred.

"Look at my eye," she told me. I tried not to freak, assuring her that what she'd taken probably was something I'd been given at an earlier date.

As her school day wore on, the pupil stayed big. By afternoon, she was concerned, and called me. I hit the phones in an attempt to discern what Atropine Sulfate was.

And I did.

It's not for people.

It's for animals.

We've got a 10-year-old golden retriever who required eye surgery a few years ago. The Atropine Sulfate was for her aftercare, prescribed in part to help relieve Bear's pain.

There's nothing on the bottle to indicate that, though. In fact, the dosage concludes with the words "as directed by a physician," rather than the more appropriate phrase "by a veterinarian." Upon learning of her error, Hollie's immediate concern was whether she should seek treatment.

Mine, naturally, was to wonder if I should exchange her Christmas presents for one of those cedar-lined doggie comforters.

An engraved set of dog dishes.

Chewy toys.

"You should talk," she said. "You're the one who tried out the electric dog collar on yourself."

Which is true. But my first-person experiment with Invisible Fence was for a column I wrote this past summer, not a medical accident.

I phoned Dan Arsulowicz, an optometrist more than 25 years now. His advice was typical, but worth repeating: "Don't use just anything on your eyes."

What people don't realize, he said, is that certain solutions are for certain conditions. If you're in doubt, call a medical expert.

Dan said he's seen or heard of folks who have injured their eyes with everything from a chunk of spaghetti to curling irons to jalapeno sauce.

"You name it," he said.

My wife needs no lectures now, of course. She's received enough reminders of her goof from me (the leash, the Milk Bones, the razzing) as well as friends and co-workers, one of whom sent her a care package containing more biscuits.

In all, it will be eight to 10 days – maybe more – before her pupil shrinks and healthy vision is restored. She's been a good sport throughout, which is far more than I could say about myself had this happened to me.

I'd share more with you, but I have to go now, as I think that's her just now arriving home.

I hear scratching at the door.

House is Full of Christmas

My wife, whom I love, has just started decorating our home for Christmas, which each year produces exactly two reactions from me:

1. Merry Christmas, everyone!

2. I'm scared.

The Grinch I'm not, but let me just suggest that sometimes, some people go a little too far with getting festive.

I like Christmas. So much so, that I find myself listening even more than usual to "The River" radio station (100.5 FM) on account of they're playing nothing but Yule music all day and all night.

Allow me to demonstrate. (Columnist goes to radio, turns volume up, hears Vanessa Williams singing "I'll Be Home For Christmas").

See? So don't say I don't enjoy the season. Especially if Vanessa Williams sings to me at lunchtime. Or, anytime.

But it would be nice to come through the front door without running smack-dab into a wreath, where 11 other months of the year, there's open hallway.

It would be nice to stretch my arms in the morning without taking out six strings of Christmas lights.

It would be nice to stroll through the house and see something – just one thing – that's not red or green.

I opened the cookie jar this morning: Christmas cookies. From the Christmas Cookie Walk held each year by the Lutheran church.

I gazed through our windows to the woods out back, and my view was completely blocked by a Santa Claus windsock. Which, if I were just a few years younger, would give me extreme nightmares, for this is a Santa without arms or legs, and he blows wildly like some ghostly apparition.

Our entire abode is festooned with mini Christmas trees. Trees of wood plastic, ceramic, cheesecloth, and I think one of them is made out of dog food.

We lie beneath Christmas quilts.

We walk beneath Christmas mistletoe.

The clock has been replaced with a version that rings out a different Christmas carol on the hour. (You don't know the joy of it all until you've heard "Up On The Housetop" every morning at 4 sharp).

We wander past tinseled railings and ascend and descend stairways decked with boughs of holly.

And speaking of boughs, it's never enough to simply cut a Christmas tree, which is huge and makes my recliner disappear from its comfy corner four weeks a year.

No. We have to collect every evergreen bough discarded by fellow tree killers.

"Just a few more," my wife says, as the children fade from view beneath armloads of prickly green branches.

There's no longer any beer in the fridge. The grates are taken up by quarts of egg nog.

My books are shoved to the back of the shelves, and subtly replaced with little gems like "The Greatest Christmas Ever." If opened, it oddly falls to page 46, which is a list of "Things your wife would love to receive at Christmas." It includes suggestions like "A trip for two to a mountainside bed and breakfast inn."

Which, last time I checked, is not available at Big Lots.

Our front yard, she leaves to me. Sort of. I string a single strand of tiny white lights against a single row of plastic garland and stand back to say "Finished."

She sighs. "Don't you want to add some boughs?"

The children extend their bleeding palms and begin to cry.

"Let's all go inside," I say, and after knocking a couple of wreaths to the floor and tripping on a string of just-strung multicoloreds, I notice something new taped to the dining room wall.

"Didn't the kids make those a few years back?" I mumble through a mouthful of Christmas Celebration-Spritz-Meltaway-Springerle cookies, and my mind wanders to Christmases past.

And gently, though it's definitely an epiphenomenal moment, I realize that with every ornament lopsidedly hung and sliver of tinsel cast helter-skelter on the tree, we're celebrating something greater than ourselves.

Subtle can be beautiful, but so too can sub-gaudy, especially if it's your partner going to so much trouble to spread cheer throughout her family.

So bring on the lights, I say, even if it means a home-equity loan for more extension cords.

But the Santa wind sock's still gotta go.

It creeps me out.

Scooch Over in the Pew

Spending time at church is supposed to be a time of prayer and praise, of rejoicing and reflection, of penance and promises.

So why instead am I stifling the urge to kick the person next to me in the keister? One reason: Poor "pew-tiquette."

I'm not sure if Miss Manners ever addressed the issue, but I sure could use her advice on what to do the next time someone sitting in the pew I've chosen makes me clamber over them so they can retain their oh-so-special position along the aisle.

The seemly thing to do is move toward the middle of a pew as soon as you arrive, and have others file in so the end seats are filled last.

But somehow, the aisle seat has ascended to a position of significance.

"People plant," says the Rev. John Hitzeroth, pastor of Peace Lutheran Church in Sparta. "And it truly crosses all denominations. There are people who just don't want to be flanked."

Hitzeroth is at a loss to explain the 'why' behind such a phenomenon. "People will gladly sit in the middle of a row at a concert where they've paid $40 for a ticket," he says, "but when it comes to church, well ..."

Chuck Howell, rector at Grace Episcopal Church in East Grand Rapids, noted that during the mid-19th century, Episcopalians and possibly others "rented" pews as a way to help finance churches.

That custom was replaced by regular pledges, but the notion of "ownership" still continues with many churchgoers who feel compelled to sit in the same spot each Sunday, he observed. "Some people are very territorial," he said, "and others are great."

I understand the need for an end position when it comes to other venues. Ask any guy which urinal he is attracted to in a public restroom, for example, and he will tell you the one mounted closest to a wall. That way, the most you can have is one neighbor, on either your right or left.

When you're in a hurry at the grocery store, you naturally gravitate toward the check-out with the least amount of people. But Sunday service isn't something you should seek to hurry from. There's no special lane for worshippers who have "10 or fewer" prayers to raise up.

Come on people, we're talking church here. Where we're supposed to celebrate as a community. Engage one another. Be neighborly.

You wouldn't know it, though, by the way some in attendance guard their precious aisle seats.

There are valid reasons, I suppose, for forcing people to make like billy goats and climb over you and your stuff. You might be cursed with an upset stomach or a weak bladder and need to bolt for the bathroom.

But not everyone sitting on the ends has diarrhea, for God's sake.

I've never conducted research, but I'll bet Bibles to Psalters the reason most people demand to stay put is simply because they're flaunting an "I-was-here-before-you-were" attitude.

Hey, we were all selfish 8-year-olds at one time.

But someday, we have to grow up and share the space.

Move over, you boorish, ill-mannered louts.

My Son's Party Has Graduated into a Spectacle

I nearly cried tears of joy when our son, set to graduate from high school next month, announced what he wanted at his open house:

Brats and root beer.

So simple. So Heartland-y. So Patrick.

But I am close to shedding tears of another sort now, since being made to realize that people attending an open house cannot survive on pork and pop alone.

It may have been true 36 years ago, when I graduated from high school and had a little get-together in my family's postage stamp-sized backyard. It featured burgers, potato salad and slaps on the back.

But, through reasons no one seems able to explain, the simple graduation party has morphed into an all-consuming drain on the family budget, the family property and the family psyche.

My wife, much smarter than I in the way of parties and throwing them, began planning Patrick's open house about 16 years ago, when he was 2.

"And wut wud widdle Patwick want for his gwaduashin party-warty?" she used to ask, cooing into his stroller.

And he'd answer, "Buh. Buh."

"The kid wants to play catch," I tried to tell her.

But Hollie, better versed in baby talk, would wave me away and, returning her gaze to the baby, announce, "Of course we'll have ponies there!"

OK, so I'm exaggerating. But not much.

Our oldest son's open house was a breeze, held in rented space and featuring simple sandwiches and a couple of side dishes.

However, I'm learning that to stage a gig for your grad on your own turf requires months of planning.

For Christmas, my better half didn't request jewelry or an ocean cruise, begging Santa Claus instead to send someone to wash our windows for the June 1 open house.

St. Nick came through, of course, which means I'm mustering the courage to ascend a 40-foot ladder armed with Bon Ami, a squeegee and my prayer book.

Then, there's the yard.

It's a venerable old plot, meaning grass doesn't root well. Unless, of course, you attack it with rakes, seed, topsoil, fertilizer, a 300-pound roller, bales of scattered straw and nightly waterings – which, "Merry Christmas, everyone!"

– I'm doing.

Never mind that herniated disc.

Although June typically is sunny, I've been told we'll also need tents, in case it rains or gets too sunny. And all that cavernous space beneath the tents looks out of place unless you cram tables and chairs in there.

"But people can eat standing up," I pleaded.

"We're out of Bon Ami," she answered, handing me a rag. "Now go."

Just last week, Hollie caught me wheezing against our wheelbarrow and asked if I could tuck a water feature into the landscape.

"You know, like a stream and a fountain and a waterfall and tons and tons of boulders," she said, casting her arms to encompass a swath of lawn about 200 feet long.

"Sure," I said cheerfully. "Soon as I finish up on the gazebo, pergola, arbor, privacy fence, bocce court, butterfly garden, statuary, putting green, granite benches, outdoor lighting, flagpole, dog run, wiffle ball field, new driveway, utility shed and outdoor kitchen."

She smiled wryly. "Don't forget the covered bridge."

We are having brats and root beer, although I'm also hearing rumors of an ice cream bar, popcorn machine, sno-cone maker and chocolate fountain. The brats are by special order, and the soda is coming in a keg and will cost close to what I spent on the only suit I own.

Not that I'll be wearing it. I have to go out and buy a shirt with a logo on it and khaki shorts that aren't stained with caulk, along with something called "Docksiders," which don't come with steel toes.

This is unfortunate, because I'll probably still be lugging rocks around the yard the morning of the party.

Not that I'm complaining.

Even in the midst of all that work, I'm staying focused.

Family and friends. A cold root beer and a brat or two.

And, if I'm really lucky – before the kid splits for Michigan State University for what I already know is going to feel like forever – one fleeting game of catch.

Color Me in Tough Pastels

The paint names "Peach Dust" and "Airy Delight" are enough to make a man blush blood red.

We're hoisting stogies and suds around a rowdy game of pinochle when Tubby blurts out, "Look like you've been doin' some paintin' in here. Ya don't see many rooms done up in red."

And from another room, the wife chirps, "Actually, the color is 'Souvenir Orchid.' More dip, anyone?"

All faces turn on me, and Tubby mouths the words "Souvenir Orchid" once more, or at least I think he's only mouthing them, on account of all I can hear is a freight train of mocking laughter from some marrow-deep place within.

That's when I wake up, my forehead beaded with perspiration and my skin as pale as . . . well, as pale as "Snow Ballet." Or "Peachdust." Or "Airy Delight."

I've embellished the nightmare. But the colors are real. They exist on little sample cards that carry paint "chips" and their respective names. You see them in decorator dens and hardware and discount and department stores – every color of the spectrum exploded into a million hues.

It wasn't always like that. I remember helping my father once paint the house in which he and my mother still reside. We went to the store and bought paint that said this on the label:

Gray.

People would go by and say, "Nice gray."

We used another color for trim. Know what it was?

White.

The same passersby would make another walk past the project and they'd nod and they'd say, "Say now, gray with white trim. That's swell."

But nowadays, the closest thing I can find to gray is "Vapor Shadow" and "Mouse House" and "Licorice" and "Flying Dove" and "Overcast."

And white isn't white anymore. It's "Dawn" and "Bridal Pink" and "Divine" and "Dewkist."

And it's why I'm so afraid to paint the room in our own home that now needs painting. Because it has come down to a choice between "Oakleigh Peach" and "Victorian Rouge" and – this is not easy to write – "Romantic Revival Moss Rose."

I am already fretting over ensuing conversations with guys who come to visit once I've got the brushes out:

"What is that; is that pink you're painting?"

"It's not pink. It's way darker, like the color of bricks. Big, heavy bricks that guys with Popeye-like arms butter up and build big buildings with."

"Looks pink to me."

"Pink is what Barbie wears. This color is like a rust color, or maybe blood. You know, bloody stuff; gladiators."

And then my friend would spy the top of the paint can. And he'd read "Dreamsicle." And I would never, ever see him again.

I think that what those of us who, sorrily, do more painting than card-playing really need is a new way of naming paint colors.

The way it's done now is pretty obvious. A bunch of women with notepads and pens gather around an absolutely huge bong and just blurt out whatever nonsense comes to mind when shown a color.

When orange is held up, for example, they yell "Little Miss Sunbeam" and "Bumblebeebuns" and "Apricot on the Windowsill." And the paint people, who have probably shaken one too many cans, nod and go, "Say now, Little Miss Sunbeam with Bumblebeebuns trim. That's swell."

What we need a little more of are paint names that reflect the other gender, so that next time Tubby asks "You finish off that gallon of "Blithe Spirit" yet, I can say, "Nah, we changed the whole color scheme and did the game room up in 'Raw Knuckles." It was a toss-up between that or "Gangrene Torte."

Now. Whose deal?

Kindergarten is Tough These Days

It's time for kindergarten at Gladiola Elementary School in Wyoming. I know this because the little hand is on the 8 and the big hand is on the 5. The teacher asks us to sit on squares on the floor.

"I'm Mrs. Weaver," she says, and starts to hand out name tags. Darla, Kelly, Jenny, Karen, Andrew, Sarah, Juanita, Carrie, Chad. Finally, Tommy. "Did everyone get a name tag?" Mrs. Weaver asks.

A boy in a blue shirt starts to cry. He didn't get a name tag. He didn't get in the right room, either. He's sobbing now, and he blurts out, "I want my mommy."

So do I. So does everyone else. But most mommies tell their kids that if they don't cry on their first day of kindergarten, you'll get a treat. Mine says don't cry because you're 35 and you'll embarrass me.

It's almost 9 and we're still sitting on squares, which is about as comfortable as surgery. I look around the room. I was never this little. Mrs. Weaver talks about the bathroom. That's good, because the boy in front of me keeps pinching his crotch.

Next we are told about room rules. Raise your hand to talk. Keep hands and feet to yourself. Work quietly at your seats. Walk in the room. No fighting at any time. This isn't kindergarten. This is a POW camp.

A girl raises her hand. "Do we get homework today?" Another girl suddenly announces that "At the red cottage, a little kitty fell down the chimney." A third girl interrupts: "We had a cat, but it didn't have a tail. But they didn't cut it off. They bought it like that."

Future newspaper columnists.

We go from the little squares to the work tables. I sit in a chair that propels my knees into my forehead. Andrew is on my left, Jason on my right. Andrew looks at me, strangely. "I'm 6," he says.

I nod.

"How old are you," he asks.

"Older than 6."

"Do you know how to drive?"

"Yes."

"Well," he counters, "I have a dog."

Mrs. Weaver gives us teddy bear pictures to color, and a box of new crayons. "Use brown," Jason tells me. Andrew leans over: "Use peach." I use every crayon in the box. I draw a Frankenstein scar on my teddy bear's forehead. It's a habit

I've got. "What's that?" Andrew asks.

"It's a Band-Aid."

"You're weird," says Andrew. "Bears don't have Band-Aids."

Bears don't have names like "Teddy," either. And they eat little boys for lunch.

It's story time. It's a story about the first day at kindergarten. In the story, everything goes pretty smoothly. Nobody pinches their crotch, that's for sure.

Next, it's recess. Andrew comes over to me. "You can't play on this stuff," he says. "You're too big."

After recess, we all get a drink. Then a lot of us go to the bathroom.

Back to the floor, says Mrs. Weaver. Andrew sits beside me. His look is stern. "You're not sitting on a square."

We do finger plays. Everyone can do them except me. After that, we get play time. Mrs. Weaver shows us toys called "Construx." She shows us "Popoids." She shows us "Unifix" cubes.

I ask where the Lincoln Logs are. I ask where I can find the TinkerToys. She says nobody plays with those.

"What about snack time? Milk and crackers?

She shakes her head. "Not any more."

"Nap time, then. When's nap time?"

"Long gone," she answers.

The little hand is on the 11. Almost time to go home. We put our stuff in knapsacks. I ask Andrew if he'll be back tomorrow. He says no.

"What are you gonna' do then?

"Play outside."

Me, too. Kindergarten's hard.

CHAPTER 3

Legacies

Harwell Still Takes Us
on Magic Carpet Ride

In 27 years of working out of the same newsroom, I've never seen anyone bring the place to a standstill like the little giant in a beret who sauntered through on Friday afternoon.

He's not a politician. Never starred in a professional sport. Hasn't got cinema by the throat, either.

The most powerful and influential man in all of Michigan has only to utter a word or two, and his public melts. People stop in mid-act. A salty newsroom buckles at the knees. ... when Ernie Harwell comes calling.

The 87-year-old Voice of Summer is a spokesman these days for a health-care concern, and was in Grand Rapids last week to promote walking and wellness. It's a good fit for a man who reportedly eats mostly fruits and vegetables, and red meat but a few times a month. It would be an even better fit if, upon retiring, we had given him the keys to the State of Michigan, and permanently housed him in the governor's mansion on Mackinac Island.

On second thought, he should have been installed as governor.

Ernie Harwell, in a word, bespeaks class.

In all the years that we have known him, that we have invited him onto our porches and into our second-shift factory jobs and alongside us on nighttime car rides and into our treehouses or tucked beneath a sheet so we could hide his voice from parents who thought getting sleep on a school night was somehow more important than tuning in, Ernie Harwell has never let us down.

Same gal forever and ever – Lulu.

Same opening poetry from the Song of Solomon to begin the sacred seasons – "For lo, the winter is past."

Same beautiful pace, slithering along the airwaves on a Georgian accent of honey-covered gravel.

What he gave us – what he continues to extend in a life after baseball – is the ability to transport any Tigers fan to another place, another time, another team.

For me, it was dialing in on a Motorola transistor radio when I should have been slumbering. Or even better, sitting with my brothers and my now-deceased father on a porch made for listening at eventide, being whisked to the corner of Michigan and Trumbull to catch up on Lolich, Cash and Kaline. Ernie was the magic carpet.

When I heard he was scheduled to be in our downtown building in just moments – my first opportunity to see him in person – I wasn't sure whether I was going to wet my pants or burst into tears, and I'm 51.

I stopped being a hero-worshipper a long time ago, but this was the person, the voice, who had helped make baseball an intoxicant, when the game was still a game.

For longer than I care to admit, I really thought he knew the hometowns of all those people who snagged foul balls.

"That one was caught by a gentleman from Mount Pleasant," Ernie would announce, and I was convinced he knew all the universe.

His love affair with people has always cut across all races, both genders.

If you were to have asked me why some of the women had a certain look in their eyes Friday, I'd have guessed the Diet Coke guy was on his way in. Shirtless.

Instead, it was a diminutive man who cannot weigh 140, walking beneath a dark beret and in a coat that seemed to hang more than it did highlight.

When he came past me, I stuck my hand out like a kid trying to hitch a ride. And maybe I was.

In an age of anxiety and plain stupidity where people stay up late and miss work because they crave to know which woman The Bachelor selected, Ernie Harwell is a bus ride back to a saner time, when we drank lemonade and fire-brewed beer.

Few people – few voices – can pilot me to a four-columned porch with 20 front slats, where my brothers and I would join my father, luxuriating in one man's every syllable.

It's my own black & white postcard – of sultry nights when fireflies owned the yews and crickets and cicadas competed with The Voice for nine timeless innings.

Last Friday, I went home again.

Ernie drove.

Jay Van Andel's Courage Shines on Dedication Day

They talk about his money and they talk about his vision.

But what Jay Van Andel displayed Wednesday was nothing less than raw courage.

Despite visibly suffering from the effects of Parkinson's disease, he made his way to the podium to address a crowd of 500 assembled to dedicate the research institute bearing his name.

And despite excruciatingly long pauses, inaudible fragments and occasional non-sequiturs, he prevailed, even managing to inject humor into a speech that those present likely will not forget.

With scarce exception, the 76-year-old Van Andel has been a philanthropist in absentia, his designees accepting countless thank-yous and accolades on his behalf. But on Wednesday, he provided a glimpse into what a struggle affairs of daily living must be – and how a determined mind does battle with an ailing body.

Another man might have stayed home. Jay Van Andel, though, chose to come forward on a day that belonged to him and his wife Betty, who suffers from Alzheimer's and did not attend.

The audience – a sea of suits reflecting a Who's Who of Grand Rapids and environs – sensed even before Van Andel began to speak what a challenge he must be enduring, and signaled admiration with an ovation that lasted more than half a minute.

The atmosphere already was steeped in symbolism and metaphor, thanks to former President Gerald R. Ford, who spoke before Van Andel did and related how "The Bible tells us that old men plant trees as an act of faith," even though they might not last to enjoy their shade.

Without mincing words, Ford then went on to indicate that Van Andel himself would not live forever – who of us can? – and later concluded his remarks by announcing "Generations yet unborn will thank God for (the Van Andels') vision, their generosity and their springtime of hope that is their legacy."

When Van Andel took the stage, his son, David, stood by. And throughout the several minutes the senior Van Andel alternately spoke and stood silent before the microphone, many wondered whether David might gently usher him back to his seat.

He did not. Rather, a son stood proudly while his father discussed the crowning achievement in his life – a gift to the world.

"Unfortunately, what a lot of people fail to realize is that my father is as sharp as ever mentally, David would explain later. "He just has trouble trying to express himself, and some days are better than others."

"Today's ceremony," is how Jay Van Andel began his talk, and after apparently losing his way, he surfaced again with "journey for our family."

The word "rewarding."

The phrase "help unravel the mysteries of disease ... of pain."

"We pray for God's blessings on this journey," he said.

Van Andel acknowledged longtime associate Casey Wondergem with a smile and remark, and at one point said "Thank you, David," when his son brought the microphone closer to the elder's faint voice.

There were long, awkward pauses, one or two of which lasted a minute. Those in the crowd quite likely were either embarrassed or uncomfortable with the lapses, which were filled in by passing traffic, and the roar of exhaust fans atop Spectrum Health Downtown.

"There was never a question whether my father would speak today," David Van Andel said. "It was his decision. I was very happy that he chose to express himself. Nobody else could have done it justice."

At one point, Jay Van Andel surprised everyone – and acknowledged his handicap in the process – when midway through his talk he blurted: "You have to understand that this is not scripted."

Waves of laughter overtook the audience, and it rippled through again when he added with a smile that his speech "won't be repeated."

In another tender moment, he simply stated "I have this disease called Parkinson's disease," and he went on to murmur the names of others so afflicted, including U.S. Attorney General Janet Reno and Palestinian leader Yassar Arafat. "The list goes on."

"It's been a dream of mine for some time," he said of the institute, and used the word "fulfilling" to describe his present sentiment.

Van Andel closed, not surprisingly, by asking that the research center be the recipient of "God's blessing."

Then, he said "thank you," and the applause was thunderous.

On trembling legs, he finally stepped forward and cut the ceremonial ribbon. Although President Ford helped steady Van Andel's left arm, the man of the hour needed no help in slicing through the silk.

If there is pathos here, it is Jay Van Andel suffers from Parkinson's, and stood Wednesday in the shadow of the very building whose scientists may discover a cure.

But Jay Van Andel's special triumph was this: In an era marked by gangs of speechwriters and public relations specialists, one man stepped forward and delivered his own imperfect voice.

'It's Been a Great Run'

On a day perfect for running, the area's premier retired high school running coach could not.

Leonard Skrycki listened instead on a speakerphone from a hospital bed where he is in the late stages of lung cancer. And his brown eyes welled with tears Wednesday as more than 300 people gathered five miles away at Richmond Park to laud him not only as West Catholic High School's longtime cross-country coach, but one superb human being.

"On a day we gather to honor heroes," said Greg Meyer, "we also gather to honor someone who impacted a lot of others' lives."

Meyer – who competed for Skrycki and went on to win the Boston Marathon – was just one of several on hand to help unveil a plaque dedicating West's home course at Richmond Park the Leonard J. Skrycki Cross Country Trail.

The bittersweet ceremony honors Skrycki as the longest-serving high school coach in any sport throughout Michigan. In all, he devoted nearly 40 years to the Falcon harrier teams, including the State Championship Team of 1970, led by Meyer.

Grand Rapids Mayor John Logie read a proclamation commending Skrycki as "a man whose character and being embodied all the positives the world has to offer."

City Commissioner Roy Schmidt – who competed against Skrycki's teams as a Union High School runner in the early '70s – added that, "You were put here for a reason – to coach kids. It was your destiny."

Through the speakerphone at Saint Mary's Mercy Medical Center, the retired coach choked back tears, and his voice crackled through the air. "It brings tears to my eyes," said the 67-year-old mentor.

Skrycki's wife, Ruthanne read a letter her husband had penned from his bed, where he remains weak and largely reliant on an oxygen mask. "I'm with you in heart, mind and spirit," he wrote. "I'm honored, and I love each and every one of you attending this dedication."

His note drew a laugh when he repeated the phrase his runners have come to know as classic Skrycki: "If ifs and buts were candy and nuts, every day would be Christmas."

It's just one of the pepper-uppers Skrycki used during his long coaching tenure to motivate kids through one of high school's most arduous sports.

"Thanks," he told the crowd, "for this lofty honor," though he reminded those present that when he meets his maker, "I want the Lord to measure with the tape around my heart, not my head."

The day before, Skrycki indulged me in a bedside interview, and he seemed to enjoy reminiscing not only about the runners he had coached, but all the simple pleasures that life has brought him.

He remembered growing up poor on the West Side he would come to love and cherish, and how his family of 11 would raise rabbits and chickens in their yard on Muskegon Avenue NW to make ends meet.

He would pick fruit for pennies per quart, and hitchhiked to the Highlands golf club to caddie for 35 cents a day. Few know the far reaches of his generous nature; for years, he raised bees to supply the Carmelite nuns with honey. He called his runners "my family."

"It's been a great run," said Skrycki, "but I guess the Lord may have other plans for me now."

Still, he has not given up on what doctors acknowledge is a terminal illness. He resumed chemotherapy on Tuesday. "I'm praying for a miracle," he said.

To close Wednesday's ceremony, an impressive plaque bearing Skrycki's image was revealed just short of the trail's finish line, and only moments before several schools took to the starting line for a cross-country meet scheduled for the same afternoon.

"Runners, come to the line," said the starter.

There was a race to run. There always will be.

It's a Tribute to Teachers

It's oh-so-quietly sandwiched between May Day and Mother's Day, a week dedicated to humble people in our midst who not only instruct our children, but who sometimes spend more time getting to know them than their parents and grandparents.

Welcome to Teacher Appreciation Week, five days set aside to honor men and women who go to school too long, earn too little, and too often suffer from the small minds that dismiss them only as "public servants."

I graduated with a teaching degree, in special education. My wife and brother and several in-laws are involved in education.

Yet I don't believe that makes me zealous to a fault. I simply choose to see teachers for what the bulk of them are: Underpaid and under-appreciated mentors who ought to be gently elevated at least one week a year.

Yes, yes, I hear you: They have their summers off.

And guess what, Homer? You could, too, had you chosen teaching as a profession. Nobody forced you to become an accountant or a chef or a tool-and-die maker. The doors to teaching colleges don't discriminate.

Bad teachers out there?

No question about it. Bad journalists, too. And bad clergy and bad homemakers and bad bartenders and bad bricklayers. My friends, there's bad all over the planet. Always has been.

Schools cost too much?

Yup. And I can't say I'm in love with every new Taj Mahal they build for our kids, either.

But that's not teachers' fault. It's our own. We largely elect boards of education, and we have the absolute right to run them out if we think they're messing up.

In nearly 26 years as a newspaperman and in and out of classrooms for stories here and stories there, I believe this: Most of the teachers in charge of your kids and mine have halos waiting.

I visited Palmer Elementary School in Grand Rapids last month, not for a story, but to visit a couple of girls who had written great letters. I wanted to tell them "Nice job," and their teacher gave me the chance.

The girls I had come to see were waiting to escort me to the classroom, and during the short time I spent with their classmates, all attention was on me, which is saying something for them, and for their teacher.

A few days later, I received a packet that included a long letter from virtually every kid. "Thanks," is the way each began, and I wondered how many moms and dads – if all the teaching were left to them – would coach their kids on such etiquette.

The same thing happened days after I visited Thornapple Elementary in Ada – a ton of letters and homespun drawings mailed to my desk.

Teachers generate that sort of attention to detail. They devise incredible challenges for their kids, too. Visit Grand Rapids Union High School sometime (my brother and some of my longtime buddies work there) if you want to see a sterling future in the faces of teenagers. And I still hear some people refer to Union as "that school where they rioted in the 60s."

Get real. Get recent.

I did a fair amount of student teaching. It wore me down to a thread. You try spending an entire day on your feet - ENTHUSIASTICALLY delivering THE SAME LESSON hour after hour to kids who might rather be anywhere else – watching movies, visiting the lakeshore, in their Camaros.

Next time you read anything, argue with eloquence, quote Shakespeare, use geometry, convey photosynthesis, appreciate Monet or play a piece by Strauss, don't spend too much time patting yourself on the back.

Behind each and every one of us who soars in ways both little and large, there's a teacher in the wings, shirtsleeves rolled to the elbows, ready to elevate the next batch.

Story in Stone

The year is 1927, and while anglers coax fish from the cerulean waters of Newaygo County's Hess Lake, Burton D. Smith is onshore, engaged in a special pursuit of his own.

It is something that he would work at for 40 years, using tools no more sophisticated than a hammer, nails and a mixing stick.

But what his hands have rendered is perhaps as much a testament to the working man and woman as any modern Labor Day celebration.

Beginning that day in 1927 – and not stopping until 1967, the year before he died at the age of 90 – Burton Smith spent part of virtually every week fashioning a home that its present owners believe is not only a geologist's dream but truly one of a kind.

"People don't just visit our house," says Tina Rosato, who lives here with husband Phil Evanzo.

"They read it."

Though the couple never met Burton Smith, they were able to resurrect fragments of his life from two grandchildren – Laurelynne Harris of Saginaw County and Noel Daniels of Arizona.

According to them, Smith had enlisted to fight in the Spanish-American War of 1898 as a 17-year-old. He was fluent in Spanish, and the Army needed translators.

He was captured, though, and served time as a POW in the Philippines. To torture Smith, his captors forced him to eat bamboo slivers, knowing that to ingest them would create lifelong gastrointestinal problems.

After his release, Smith made his way to Michigan, met and married his wife, Maude, and bought the Hess Lake home in 1917.

A decade later, it would begin to undergo a transformation, thanks to Smith, who made his living as an accountant for, among others, many of the muck farmers in the area.

Because of the torture he had endured, he wasn't able to spend his free time engaging in vigorous activity, so he decided to change his home's complexion, one day at a time.

He struck on the idea of collecting stones – from lakes, rivers, outcroppings – wherever. And he hardly contained his search to Newaygo County.

Instead, he solicited help from friends, relatives and acquaintances who would travel not only the States, but to other countries, other continents.

Meanwhile, he set to work building simple frames of wood to serve as cement forms. They measured from just under to well over a square foot.

Smith would set each frame onto a flat surface, then pour a thin layer of sand. Next, he imbedded pebbles – laid as a mirror image – to spell out the geographic source of the larger stones that also would be put into the frame.

With everything in place, Smith would hand-mix cement, pour it over his rocky arrangement, then allow the whole piece to dry.

The end result, after knocking the frame from the concrete and brushing off the sand, was a block from which protruded the rocks, as well as the words wrought from pebbles.

Course by course, Smith mortared his homemade blocks to the exterior of the Hess Lake abode.

Today, the entire first floor bears his painstaking work, as does the sun porch, two fireplaces and the three-story chimney.

To view his handiwork is to tour the globe. Stones announce themselves from Lost River, N.H.; Schoenbrunn, Germany; Austria; Labrador; New Guinea; France; Wales; Harrington, England; Puget Sound; Iceland; the Black Hills; Ontario – as well as too many Michigan locations to mention.

The home sports some other idiosyncrasies, as well, including a basement wall insulated with 88 Kelvinator refrigerator doors.

Smith's grandson, Noel Daniels, 49, recalls his grandfather as a splendid artist, and in more than one medium.

"He was very good in oils," Daniels says, noting that Smith painted an exquisite copy of Frederic Remington's "The Dash For Timbers," to name just one.

"He taught himself how to do things," says Daniels, who served six years as finance director for the Grand Rapids Symphony before moving west in 1996 to work as business manager for the Phoenix Theatre.

His sister, Laurelynne, 53, recalls her grandfather as "a character" yet "brilliant."

She adds that upon returning from the POW camp with a slight tremor, Smith was forced to switch his dominant hand from right to left. Still, he was able to master painting. And she remembers that his handwriting was "like calligraphy."

Neither grandchild knows exactly what prompted Smith to cast so many blocks of cement and stone. "I think he just experimented with the process," says Daniels, "and looked to what others (masons and farmers) in the area had done."

Regardless the source of inspiration, Rosato and Evanzo couldn't walk away from the home when they visited the site in April of 1996.

"We had come up here not intending to buy anything," she remembers. "But we bought that very day. We fell in love with the story."

Evanzo, 61 and a retired postmaster from Comstock Park, has extensively remodeled the home's interior. But he sidestepped Smith's work at nearly every turn.

"I did everything I could to keep the exposed stone clear," he recalls. "The only place I took stones away is when I installed sliding glass doors."

Even then, Evanzo was careful to re-use those stones, moving them to the water's edge, where he laid in a modest seawall.

Perhaps equally remarkable to Smith's feat is the apparent fact that, until now, his work had never been the object of a formal news report.

"No (journalists) have shown any amazement at this, as far as we can tell," says Rosato, 54, formerly a free-lance writer with the Grand Rapids Foundation.

Mostly true. However, Laurelynne Harris recalls that many years ago, Life magazine approached the family about doing a story on the home.

Smith would have nothing of it. According to Harris, her grandparents answered the magazine's request by responding, "Fools' names and faces appear in public places."

Rosato and Evanzo say they've been more than willing to share what they call their "sleepy little treasure."

"Just the other day," says Rosato, "a car drove past, and we heard brakes screeching. "They couldn't believe it. They were amazed. They stayed a half hour."

Neighborhood Helper Was Born With Gift of Lifelong Innocence

When David Schultheiss was born some 46 years ago, the tiny bundle didn't include a scholar's aptitude or the creative genius of an artist or composer.

Instead, he was endowed with something far greater – a sense of selflessness. An affinity for sparrows. The love of libraries and a kinship with children.

David Schultheiss was given the gift of lifelong innocence.

Too many know him only as the man who lumbers along sidewalks in the Riverside Park area and, depending on the season, either pushes a tired old lawn mower or shoulders a snow shovel.

It's but a thin sliver of the man who still resides with his parents – they're both approaching 82 – just a stone's throw from the river Grand.

David has been tending various lawns and sidewalks in his neighborhood nearly every day since 1971, so nearly 30 years.

It's not yet 8 a.m. when he announces, "All set, all set," after arranging his workday gear.

He carries a pair of one-gallon gas jugs on the rusty bars of the mower. A quart of oil rests on the front of the small mowing deck. He bundles up an armful of tools in a weathered plastic bag that has so many holes in it, a wrench or screwdriver will fall out at least every 100 feet or so.

"C'mon you guys," he says to the hardware. "Stay in there, stay in there. Oh, I gotta get a new bag sometime."

He heads east along Knapp Street NE. "Oh, gee, see how brown that is," says David, surveying his customers' sun-baked yards.

He is dressed in a blue T-shirt, cap and oversized denim shorts smeared with signs of his work: grease, gas, oil and grime. He wears blue dress socks and black sneakers. He will cut four yards today.

First, though, he will allow himself to be awed by birds. "Awww, look at them sparrows," he says, sounding a lot like Lennie in Steinbeck's classic tale "Of Mice and Men."

"They're so darn cute," says David, drawing to a complete halt. "Lookit that, lookit that; they're not hardly afraid. So cute. So cute."

His first job is around the corner on Dean Street. He checks his fuel tank. It's nearly full. Still, he is meticulous about adding perhaps a half cup of gas to top it off just right.

After one pass, he adjusts the choke, which is constantly slipping. He shaves a patch of grass, being careful not to disturb a proud stand of foxgloves.

When he's finished the front and back, Doris Jingles meets him on the back stoop. She is 77 and a General Motors retiree. David has been cutting her grass for nearly 20 years, and she once gave him a "Born To Mow" baseball cap.

Back in 1980, David charged her $3.50. "I tried paying him five dollars once," says Doris, "but his mother called me up and said, 'The price is three-fifty.'"

And so it is, still.

"He's wonderful," says Doris. "He's a Christian, and he loves Jesus."

The sun is climbing when David pulls up to Martin Downey's home. "David does a real good job," says Martin, and he pays the lawn mower man before heading off to work at Rogers Department Store.

Finished with the Downey yard, David ambles down the sidewalk. He meanders left and right a little, mumbles a bit to himself as he goes, and, as always, is on the lookout for birds.

"I like this next place," says David. "The sparrows there are really friendly. And so cute. So cute."

He removes the sparkplug – "Real dirty," he says – and cleans it with the front of his shirt. "There," he says, replacing it.

Jan Sinkler calls out from a second-story window. "Let it go today," she tells David. He is just getting along when she emerges from the front door.

David wheels. "Where's your daughter that had the baby?" he asks. "Where's she living?" Then he asks about another daughter. "How's Jane doing?"

Jan Sinkler shakes her head in appreciation. "He's terrific," she says of her helper. "Faithful. Wonderful. I love him."

So do David's parents. Their love is what prompted them to ignore advice from medical specialists at the time who suggested they institutionalize him.

"You just don't do that with someone you love," says Faye, taking a seat on the couch of the home where she grew up.

David enters the living room. He sits beside her and takes her hand and stares off with a crooked smile.

"We wanted someone to pray with him at night before he went to sleep," she remembers thinking of the decision she made in concert with Fred, who still works part time as a machinist.

It was the right thing to do, says Faye, recounting all the blessings David has provided them – and others.

"So many people have been so patient with him," she says. "They seem to understand his situation."

Some haven't, of course. David bristles slightly when recalling teens that have infuriated him with their teasing. He doesn't provide details. Just says "Not so bad, now."

When he's not mowing or shoveling, David visits nearby Briggs Park or revels in cheering on teams competing in the Northern Little League at Riverside Park. He's endeared himself to so many there that the League presented him with a trophy.

It's inscribed with a single word: "Superfan."

He visits area libraries, often relying on the bus, which he mastered with little trouble. And he thrills to organ music. He's attended concerts at several churches, including his own – Second Congregational on Cheshire Drive NE, where senior minister M. Bruce Irwin says, "Church almost wouldn't be church without David there."

David is the sixth of seven born to the Schultheisses. The others are grown and married and gone, though provisions are in place for them to care for their brother when it's time.

Meanwhile, David – still dressed in his work clothes – seems perfectly content to rest on the couch, smiling slightly. He is clutching his mother's tiny hand. He glances out a window facing north.

One more perfect day for watching sparrows.

17-Year Journey is More Than Just a Bike Ride

When you have a penchant for something healthy and of value, then there is every reason to pursue that goal, that dream.

For Mel and Loren VanFarowe, they have nibbled away at such a quest one Saturday morning at a time, pedaling their way down every single street in Kent County.

It is an odyssey that began 17 years and nearly 6,000 miles ago, way back in 1979.

What makes their journey perhaps even more remarkable is that they've achieved their goal on a rather bland one-speed tandem.

And this: That Mel's son Loren has never seen a single thing along the way. He has been blind since birth.

"I just thought it up with my dad 'cause I really like to go bicycling," says Loren, who's 39 and lives with parents Mel and Emaline on the city's Southeast Side.

The duo's extended jaunt actually began as an attempt to ride down every Grand Rapids city street. That took two years. "Then, we just had the idea of doing the whole county," says Mel, who's 68.

So they traversed every road in every city in the county, as well as county roads and blue highways - everything but expressways, which aren't open to bikes anyway.

"We would get up at 4:30 or 5 o'clock," says Loren, addressing the Saturday mornings they rode. Lately, though, they've been sleeping in. " 'Till 6 or 6:30," says Loren.

Friday nights, they'd consult a dog-eared county map Loren kept in a dresser drawer. By dawn the next day, they'd be making their mark on the world, a forest green Schwinn Twinn carrying father and son down roads the rest of us fly along in our autos.

Mel, a retired educator, says the streets they covered rarely failed to satisfy. "People don't realize how beautiful Kent County is. We're thankful to God for that beauty, and for the health we had and the strength He gave us along the way."

That's not to say there weren't interruptions. Mel underwent triple bypass heart surgery in the fall of 1989. It grounded him only six weeks.

There were other groundings, though, including an end-over-end spill on loose gravel in Caledonia Township that left both VanFarowes bruised and bleeding.

But none of their half-dozen or so mishaps sent either to the hospital. Typically, they just dusted themselves off and hopped back on.

They count safety helmets among their gear, but little else. No fancy pants with chamois insets or biking shoes or even gloves or pedal clips.

Mel smiles and shrugs, as if to say, "We don't need that stuff."

They never hurried, either. "We weren't out to set any speed records," says Mel, who figures the twosome averaged 15 to 25 miles per session.

They rode through rain, and without ponchos. They rode in winter, sparingly. They rode on tar so hot it sizzled and beneath tree-covered roads that reminded them of cathedrals.

And as of today, they have just a half mile left to do, a bite-sized stretch along Kent County's northern boundary, 22 Mile Road.

They'll pedal it this coming Saturday, then host a breakfast for friends and fellow members of Shawnee Park Christian Reformed Church at Grant Christian School, just across the county line.

Grant Christian is a four-room school where the elder VanFarowe served from 1954 to 1959 as teacher, principal, bus driver, coach and a little bit of everything else.

It's also near the home in which the VanFarowes resided when Loren was born, the second of three children.

"Those were good years," says Mel, who moved his family to Grand Rapids in 1976.

These will be remembered as good years, too, he knows, years recalled as those which allowed him to share a bond tighter than most fathers and sons will ever know.

He will reminisce about how they didn't do much talking while they rode, but how from time to time, he asked his blind son if he could hear that cardinal, or the rooster crowing.

He will remember seeing deer, and slowing, and whispering to Loren that the does were just ahead, standing in the road, and that if he listened well enough, he might hear them bound away.

And finally, Mel VanFarowe might chuckle to remember how a newspaper columnist, in struggling to chronicle their adventure, erred in assuming that his son, Loren, never saw "a single thing along the way."

Mel knows better, that they have seen it all, and more importantly, beheld each other.

Mother Promises to Preserve Mural where Late Son left His Mark

She has crayon and watercolor drawings from his elementary days.

The macaroni ornament he fashioned for the family Christmas tree.

A little plaster imprint of his hand.

And so it is with a breaking heart that Mary-Ann Meyer wrestles with the possibility that the City of Grand Rapids might rule that one of the last things her son ever helped to create is a violation of the law – the gigantic painting adorning the south side of the Brass Works Building.

Just a week after Mary-Ann's 21-year-old son, Jesse, finished putting his brush to the stunning work, he was killed in a one-car accident outside his hometown of Sparta.

"When I saw the finished product, I stared at it in amazement," says Mary-Ann, 45. "I was so proud of it, and so was Jesse."

Since the 60-foot high silhouette of a foundry worker and the words "BRASS WORKS BUILDING" were rendered, however, questions have surfaced whether the work violates the city's zoning ordinance.

At issue is whether it's a mural, in which case it can stand as is – or if it's a commercial sign, in which case it's arguably too large for the side of the building to qualify as such without a variance.

Sam Cummings, a developer of the building on Monroe Avenue NW, repeated Monday that the painting "was designed to celebrate the history" of the building, and that "the mural has nothing to do with the current use" of the structure, which is to house commercial ventures.

But in a 6-2 vote late last month, the city's Zoning Board of Appeals decided that the painting did indeed qualify as "signage," and thus was subject to the more stringent requirements. Moreover, the Board could not agree that the painting met the requirements for a variance. At the same meeting, the issue was tabled.

Tomorrow, Cummings and partner Eric Wynsma will ask the Board to consider reversing its initial decision to declare the work a sign.

The $12,000 work, which boasts the image of an industrial foundry worker laboring beneath a golden spark, was designed jointly by downtown firms Gould Design and Hanon-McKendry, said Cummings.

The actual painting was performed by Clark Painting on Four Mile Road NE.

At the time, both Mary-Ann's ex-husband, Gary Cooper, 46, and their late son, Jesse, were employed by Clark, and the two spent time together on ladders and mechanical lifts, bringing the initial drawings to life.

"The last year, I got to work with him a lot, and it was a pleasure to work with my son," said Gary Cooper. "He didn't like to paint inside walls, but he enjoyed being up in the air and outside."

Jesse was something of a paradox. He attended an alternative school, but graduated in 1996 as salutatorian. He'd had run-ins with the law – mostly alcohol-related – yet was well-known, and liked. Scores attended his funeral.

"He was both a handful, and a lot of fun," his father said. "He was searching for his identity, and I think he was getting close."

"Jesse would do anything for anybody," his mother said. After high school, he experimented with different kinds of jobs, and after painting the Brass Works Building, quit to do construction for Pioneer Inc. Tragically, Jesse's mother herself raced to the scene of her son's death without knowing he was the victim.

She works as a volunteer with the Sparta Fire Department and answered the early morning call from the Sparta home she shares with Jesse's stepfather, Skip. Jesse had been southbound on Sparta Avenue when his Pontiac Fiero left the road, crossed a curb, slid across a yard and struck a tree, say Kent sheriff's deputies. He was pronounced dead at the scene.

Mary-Ann's grief has been compounded by the fact that she lost her father, Bob Hinz, just six weeks prior to losing her boy. And three weeks after her son's March 12 death, she buried Jesse's 18-year-old dog, Rowdy – on what would have been Jesse's 22nd birthday.

So fiercely does Mary-Ann feel that her son's handiwork should endure, she says she'd be willing to climb into a mechanical lift herself and paint over the letters, thus transforming it from a sign to a mural.

"I would rent the lift and paint over the letters myself, if that's what would make them happy," says Mary-Ann, who somewhat ironically, owns the "Signs & Wonders" sign shop in Rockford.

"My boy died, and I want it to stay."

Since his death, Mary-Ann says she has visited Jesse's grave site daily. It's there that she tells him, "I'll do everything I possibly can to keep the painting there. It's his legacy. It's his mark."

She has driven, too, into downtown Grand Rapids to visit her son's work. "At first, I just sat there for the longest time. Then I walked over to it, and touched it, and it was like touching Jesse again, because his hands had been there.

"And then I started crying. But I cry a lot these days."

We all knew Van Andel, but how about McLaughlin?

He trotted about the world in yachts and private jets, enjoyed vacations ashore a Caribbean island he largely called his own.

She liked playing cards with her grandsons.

His life played out in the limelight and was fraught with the finer things that only millions could provide: palatial homes, classic cars, tropical plants thriving alongside a dome-topped swimming pool.

She grew up on a farm, picked cucumbers to pay for school clothes, later worked at a bus station, a library, a retail store.

But death plays no favorites and, as fate would have it, their bodies succumbed to natural causes on the same day, Dec. 7, within hours of each other.

One – that of Jay Van Andel – would play host to hundreds of visitors expressing their final respects.

A wall – and a world – away, lay a woman named Juanita Marie McLaughlin, dressed elegantly in a black turtleneck.

What played out earlier this month at Zaagman Memorial Chapel was a study in contrasts, as employees there arranged services for two lives well lived – a billionaire and a woman whose life was defined by far more subtleties.

"She never lost sight of the simple life she came from," observed the widow's only son, Pat, who directs an insurance firm in Hudsonville.

While Jay Van Andel's obituary and services were strictly orchestrated by a team of public relations specialists, Juanita's life was shared through a grandson who penned her memoirs when he was a fourth-grader.

Juanita was born to dairy farmers near Jackson. She learned under the same female teacher for eight consecutive years while attending Smith Country School, a one-room elementary heated by a woodstove.

Saturday nights found her attending free movies projected against the outside wall of the local grocery.

She was one of 27 students graduated in 1936 from Union City High School south of Battle Creek.

She was accepted to the school of education at Western Michigan University, but couldn't attend because her frugal father refused to let her borrow money for tuition.

While Jay Van Andel also came from humble beginnings, he spent his formative years building Amway and other businesses with lifelong partner and fellow billionaire-to-be Rich DeVos.

Juanita worked as a secretary. Helped publish a cookbook for the Ladies Aid Society. Waited more than two years for her husband to return, badly wounded, from both the assault on Normandy and the Battle of the Bulge.

Van Andel served the Republican Party, the Christian Reformed Church, and all their attendant conservatism. He was on a first-name basis with presidents, heads of state.

Juanita and her disabled husband, John, were Catholic and active in the Democratic Party. They loved to dance, and once met Gregory Peck.

When Jay Van Andel's wife, Betty, preceded him in death earlier this year, he paid particular attention to how some of his millions would continue to be parceled out to charities following his passing.

After Juanita's husband died in 1972, she took a job managing a ladies retail clothing store. After 44 years in Battle Creek, she moved to Grand Rapids and joined St. Stephen Church here to be near family. At St. Stephen, about 80 people came to pay their final respects then attend her Mass.

Jay Van Andel was buried in a private ceremony, attended by family. Security guards stood by, a source said.

Juanita was laid to rest a mile from the farmhouse in which she grew up, at Sherwood Township Cemetery in Branch County. The cemetery sexton, 82-year-old Lester Diamond, was a childhood friend of hers.

When Lester was 5, he suffered a terrible gash to a main artery when his father's Model T crashed in front of Juanita's home. Juanita's parents attended to his wound.

Lester recalled that story just days after burying his hometown friend by hand, one shovelful at a time. He cried when asked to recall her life. "She was a very nice person," he said. "A wonderful person."

He did not apologize for his tears.

"It's kind of natural," he said, "especially when you knew somebody."

Super Sub: Students Pay Homage

Ralph Simms has spent 52 years as a teacher and coach, but it's likely his legacy will be as "The Substitute."

That's how proposed T-shirts bearing his image will identify a gentleman who, in subbing for more than 21 years, has endeared himself to so many high school students that they have initiated a Facebook page for him titled "I Love Mr. Sims!!"

The last time I checked, it had 1,284 friends, including an astonished young woman from British Columbia who wrote: "Mr. Simms. Holy CRAP, does he have fans or what? IS HE LOVED AROUND THE GLOBE OR SOMETHING!!!!???Well...God bless this little dude."

Is he the smartest guy in every case to step in? Probably not. He's also a little forgetful. And he's apt to dust up his trademark sweater vest with chalk.

But his respect for students, coupled with a teddy bear-like persona, make him a class favorite. Significantly, he's rarely the butt of jokes reserved for other subs.

"He's so nice, it's hard to be mean to him," says Olivia Jones, 14, an East Grand Rapids High sophomore. "He's really cute. And he gives us things that we can use in the real world."

"I seriously love Mr. Simms soo much!" a student named Lori Beth wrote on the Simms Facebook site. "I take pics of him all the time when he subs...I wish he was my grandpa."

"Truly a legend," says Dan Graham, who taught for 34 years and now is the district energy manager for EGR Public Schools. "Kids love him."

So popular is Simms that Rockford senior Taylor Russ created a caricature he plans to market on T-shirts. "He's one of the most-loved guys ever," Russ says.

Simms will be 80 in September, one of very few subs active at that age, says Scott VanLente, of Professional Educational Services Group in Caledonia, which fills sub slots in 25 Michigan counties.. "Most definitely in the top 2 percent."

"Every year, he says this is the year," Ralph's wife says of retirement, and this year is no different.

"I think this is it," Simms told me.

That would be disappointing to legions of students, though he has certainly earned full retirement. He grew up a poor kid in Little Falls, N.Y., during the Great Depression. His mother died three months after he was born, and he lived with a grandmother who was so frugal she would serve him bean sandwiches, then use the dregs from the can a day or two later for a watery soup.

Some of his fondest boyhood memories include simply "taking Sunday walks" with an uncle.

He graduated high school in 1947, later served two years during the Korean War on Okinawa, then attended MSU for two years.

At one point, he drove a '35 Chevy to Michigan and, after the vehicle drew its last breath, his right thumb got him as far as a YMCA in Lansing, where he lived for a while. He later hitched his way to Mt. Pleasant, where he earned a math degree at Central Michigan University.

While working as a doorman in a movie theater, he met the candy girl. He and Joyce married in 1952.

Simms first taught and coached in Clio. In 1960, he began 27 years at EGR High, where he taught math and coached freshman football, JV basketball and varsity baseball.

He could have hung it up years ago. The reason he hasn't boils down to one word: "kids."

"Teaching has been so rewarding," says Simms, who lives in EGR. "And it keeps me current and up to date. The kids treat me with the same respect I treat them."

For $75 a day, Simms shows up early, sporting a tie beneath his button-down sweater vest and carrying an armload of worksheets in case the regular teacher hasn't left a lesson plan.

Of course, sometimes, he just punts, and the kids know it.

"He came into my Spanish class and pretended he knew Spanish, lol," Rockford student Josh Bell told Facebook.

Another Rockford student, Jessica Stokes, wrote that, once, during a discussion of vitamins, Simms complained his wife wouldn't let him have liver, which "made a pretty boring hour highly entertaining."

If students go too far, Simms has his defenders. When a kid taped an action figure to Simms' back, "people got pissed," one student told Facebook.

Student Mark Hunt calls Simms "a funny man," and tells how a couple of years ago, The Substitute had to keep tugging up his trousers.

Simms used it as an opportunity to teach, telling the kids, "When you get old, two things tend to drop – your memory and your pants."

Their Little Angel

Muriel Kroeze knows – or at least hopes – that when she is reunited with the angel taken from her arms 50 years ago this month, he'll still be a 2-year-old boy.

He'll bump his head on heaven's tables, skin his knees, make a mess with his dessert – and Muriel will make up for half a century by embracing every moment, rejoicing to be together again, and this time, eternally.

For now, though, she and her husband Andrew, both 73, draw comfort from a short list of memories – and a handful of photos of their child, one of which they shared with the rest of us in Wednesday's Press.

In nearly 20 years of writing, I can't remember ever delving into the section we publish titled "In Memoriam" for a story's sake. But these circumstances were too tender, the text too moving. And the photo just too compelling to ignore.

Muriel said she and Andrew "were almost a little embarrassed" to remember their son in such a public way. But since doing so, they've had numerous calls from strangers, both touched and curious, to know more about a boy who died in 1950.

Andrew and Muriel met in her hometown of Chicago, and married in '46. He was fresh out of the Navy. William was born in March 1948, taking the name already shared by both parents' fathers. They called him Billy from the start.

Folks lived simply then, happily too. The American Dream flourished, but not all at once. 'We couldn't even get an apartment," Muriel remembers. "You'd put your name on lists, but there just weren't any available."

The three of them lived with Muriel's folks in a South Side flat. Muriel worked as a comptometer operator, figuring payroll amounts. Andrew signed on as a service department worker with Sears.

In the evenings, Billy would watch for dad's car to arrive, and when he spotted it, would yell a hurrah and bolt for the front door. Andrew would bound up the eight or 10 steps that led to the same entrance, and they'd meet open-armed, father embracing son.

Billy loved riding on his parents' shoulders. And listening to homemade stories, including one called "I Hear In The Air."

The title of that one is entered in Billy's baby book, a little journal that chronicles his birth weight (6 pounds, 15 ounces), length (21 inches) and eyes ("big & blue").

Ensuing pages speak to when he held his head up, at what age he sat, walked and talked (first word 'mama"). When the book asks what playmates were invited to his third birthday, however, and begs for a snapshot, the pages go cold.

"Only a couple years," Muriel manages. "And then, he was gone."

It started with flu-like symptoms, including a high fever. A trip to the doctor didn't help much. Billy was restless, crying. That night, when Andrew bounded up the steps, it was Muriel who met him. Billy was worsening. They rushed to Englewood Hospital in a '48 Plymouth.

Reluctantly, they left him there overnight. Parents weren't allowed bedside then. "Get a good night's sleep," the nurses said. Their boy was crying "Mommy, mommy" as they walked out. When Andrew and Muriel called the next morning, they were advised to return. Quickly.

He died of a ruptured appendix. The doctor who performed unsuccessful surgery was so overwhelmed by the death, he quit practicing. That evening, Andrew and Muriel climbed the steps together, alone.

Reality settled in slowly. "I would wake up at night," Muriel remembers, "and think I'd hear him crying." Then she'd take her turn.

Shortly after Billy's death, they moved here, Andrew's birthplace. They lived 37 years in a house on Nixon Avenue NW, and have spent the last six months in a Walker condominium.

Andrew stayed on with Sears for 47 years, retiring in 1986. Muriel spent 16 years as a cashier at Blodgett Memorial Medical Center. After Billy, Muriel had an ectopic pregnancy that resulted in a miscarriage. Unable to have any more biological children, the couple later adopted two daughters. Both survive, Barb and Joan.

"We didn't want to have a house without children," Muriel said.

Remembering Billy – living with the inexorable image of a bubbly 2-year-old that once dominated their lives – is alternately comforting and just plain tough.

"I think that in life, you remember the sadness more than you do the joy," Andrew says. "I can remember my wedding day, for instance, but not with the same details" – he stops in mid-sentence – "of this."

Andrew and Muriel, who belong to Westview Christian Reformed Church, say their faith has steadied them. "We know he's in heaven," says Muriel, "and we're just so glad the Lord loaned him to us for the little while we had him."

Billy – they have never called him anything else – would have turned 50 two days ago. His parents flirted once or twice with a memoriam at other junctures, but decided to act this time. "Fifty is special," says the little boy's mom. "Half a century, you know."

They have received calls from both close friends and strangers since Billy's endearing photo ran two days ago. One woman grieving her own loss would like to visit. Before hanging up, she asked, "Are tears OK?"

The Kroezes said come on over and cry.

"If putting Billy's picture in the paper can make a difference, then we're glad," says Muriel. "Maybe we might be able to do a lot of witnessing. However the Lord needs us."

Not long ago, Andrew was at a local mall and watched a mother holding her youngster. "He looked so much like Billy. I was never tempted so much as to say to that mother, 'Treat him good. You only have one chance to raise him.' "

He walked away.

And shared this instead.

CHAPTER 4

Lore

'Everyone in this Town Lost a Brother, a Son, a Loved One'

You only had to meet Jimmy Gerken once.

In the time it took to shake your hand – or, as was more to his liking, embrace – Jimmy became your instant friend. And for all time.

Gerken, the affable, huggable, teddy bear of a man-cub who roamed the campus and athletic fields of East Grand Rapids as though he owned them – and no one would argue that in ways, he did own them – died Wednesday morning after battling pneumonia.

It's a tough loss for a school district whose athletic and academic teams aren't used to defeat, especially when it involves their favorite son. A pall hung over the district Wednesday afternoon as news spread of his death at Spectrum Health's Blodgett Campus, where he was in intensive care since late last week.

In every hallway at the high school, someone was remembering. Secretaries, teachers, counselors cried. By noon, a memorial was erected in the front lobby – photos of their beloved Jimmy, and a giant paper roll that absorbed written farewells from men and women in high and low places. And the best notes came from scores of students:

"I know I only knew you for one semester," wrote Kat VanderWeele, "but your never-ending smile will always remain in my heart."

Added Becca B., Class of '02: "I love you and will miss you terribly. Always and forever."

East's high school principal broke down sobbing: "Jimmy Gerken was more important than anyone who's ever walked through these doors," said Patrick Cwayna, fighting back tears just moments after learning of Jimmy's death.

"I've dreaded the day this might happen. I always said I didn't want to be the principal. But I am, and it's harder than I ever could have imagined. Everyone in this town lost a brother, a son, a loved one today in Jimmy Gerken.

"He belonged to everybody."

Cwayna's grief was compounded by the fact that he and wife Rosalyn's oldest son, Casey, 25, was Jimmy's touring pal. At the school's home football games, Casey and Jimmy commandeered a golf cart and ran errands for the Pioneer squad and its coaches, roaring up and down the sidelines, the wind in their hair.

"A great person with a big heart," said Casey Cwayna recalling how he and Jimmy would head out for ribs, for a Whitecaps game, to celebrate a rare form of friendship. "I loved his good attitude, his sense of humor."

Although moderately mentally impaired from birth and unable to drive a vehicle or even read well, Jimmy made an indelible mark on virtually everyone he touched – with his love, his verve, his trademark hugs. His official title was that of team manager and school custodian, but in truth, he filled more roles than an employment agency – ambassador, mentor, role model, fan, neighbor, friend.

He turned 52 earlier this month, but he acted more like an excitable teen-age school kid, full of energy and unyielding optimism. He rarely stopped moving – from side to side on his feet, and with one or both hands constantly adjusting the bill of his baseball cap.

"He just always assumed he was the same age as the high school kids," said Jimmy's mother, Marjorie, as she and husband Donald sat in their home 100 yards from East's athletic field. They moved there so Jimmy could be within walking distance of his beloved Pioneers.

His bedroom hasn't been altered much since he entered the hospital last Thursday. It's a room just 9 feet by 9 feet, decorated with U-M, MSU and Notre Dame items. The pillowcase features baseball players. The sheets boast logos from sports teams. A Garfield the Cat clock graces the east wall.

Jimmy spent most of his time at home in the basement, though, where he feasted on a large collection of Western movies and sports videos. He simultaneously worked three remote controls from the large blue recliner where he sought respite from the rigors of attending to the needs of an entire school district.

Choking back tears, his parents recalled how a doctor encouraged them to place Jimmy in an institution shortly after his birth in 1950. "We were told to send him out East and forget about him," Donald said.

Their decision to the contrary would ultimately affect thousands – athletes and students and teachers and coaches and administrators who looked forward to starting their schooldays with a strong cup of Jimmy Gerken.

When George Barcheski was hired as East's football coach more than 30 years ago, one of the voices he heard on his first day on the job was that of Jimmy's.

"I'm your football manager," Jimmy said. Then he grinned. "I know where all the footballs are."

When "Bar" was hospitalized with heart trouble just before he retired, Jimmy found his way to a restricted area of the hospital.

"How'd you get in here?" Bar asked.

Jimmy grinned. "I just opened all the doors."

The two became like father and son, and Barcheski, too, wept to hear of Jimmy's death. "I don't know if I've ever met a more decent human being in my life," he said. "East lost a part of its legacy today. I just loved the guy. I don't know what I'm going to do now."

East's athletic director, Jerry Fouch, mourned similarly: "One of his great attributes was that he was your best friend. When you talked with him, you had his undivided attention."

Fouch also lauded Jimmy for the lessons he imparted on students and staff. "He'd get so upset if we lost an athletic event, but then he'd get over it and go forward, and I think he taught a lot of us how to do that.

"I'm going to miss his smile in the morning that started my day," Fouch said. "He was the smile of East Grand Rapids."

He also was "Kabookie," or "Bookie," a nickname ascribed to him by former East athletes, including EGR All-American Garde Thompson, who graduated in 1983.

Garde remembers Jimmy's early years, when Jimmy would make his way to East's games and fire an underhand shot from half-court. More times than not, he'd make it, and the cheer was deafening.

Fifteen years ago, prominent EGR businessman Peter Secchia invested more than $200,000 to build a fitness center at East, where his four children attended. Some thought that the center would be named for Secchia himself. But when the project was unveiled, it bore Jimmy Gerken's name, and Jimmy wept.

"He embodied the spirit of sports," Secchia said Wednesday. "Nobody worked harder than Jimmy to make kids believe that they had the opportunity and heart to succeed."

East Grand Rapids School Superintendent James Morse stood near where students were signing the rolled card in the high school lobby. He described Jimmy as a person immersed in "unconditional love."

There may never be, however, a way to capture Jimmy Gerken's true essence. Some see him soaring, heaven-bound, winking at the gods of love and sports. If there are angels in this afterlife, they are flapping their wings, but they are having trouble getting airborne. They're not sure how to hug.

Jimmy Gerken is giving lessons.

Ace's Landing Reminds Us How We Used To Fish

There are fish stories about the one that got away, and then there are fish stories about once upon a time, and this is one of those, revolving around an era when fishermen simply wrapped themselves in old clothes, grabbed a can of worms, woke their kids up before dawn, and went fishing.

Went fishing, that is, in little rental rowboats with no motor.

For 50 years now, that is how men and women and their young have approached Ace's Landing, a quiet nook nestled along the south bank of Wabasis Lake, a prime hideout for bass and bluegills in northeast Kent County.

At Ace's Landing, they still rent rowboats, a rare and fading tradition in the face of an era marked by so many fishermen owning their own motorized craft.

In 1951, just $1 bought you the right to row a boat all day and all night at Ace's. There was running water available from an old pump, and two shacks out back answered nature's call.

As a kid growing up in the '60s, I remember going to Ace's with my late father and my Uncle Bob, who would hand-roll his own cigarettes with Bugler tobacco, and when my father wasn't looking, let me sneak a puff or two.

Adjacent to where they kept the boats, you could buy a Coca-Cola or an orange or grape Nehi soda or a bottle of Bubble Up for 10 cents. Ace Wisinski – his real name was Winchell – would fill the great red cooler with 50 pounds of ice each Friday to keep the drinks cold all weekend.

Ace died in '79, and his wife, Alma, four years later, but their stepdaughter, Vonda, and her son, Patrick, helped me resurrect those memories just last week, when I went to revisit the landing I'd not been to in maybe 35 years.

The annual bass season opened this weekend, and Vonda, who now runs the landing with husband Mike, was busy getting the boats and docks and seat cushions ready.

But it's not the same, and she said so. "We used to have cars lined up here for the bass opener as far as you could see," she said. "Guys would wait hours for the chance to rent one of the boats, and we'd rent all 40 of 'em three and four times over again.

"Sometimes, they'd come for bullhead at night, or to hunt turtles. Some of the trucks would be just filled with turtles." Entire clans, she said, would convene at Ace's Landing to rent a boat, maybe loll about on the shore with soft drinks and sandwiches, spend time as a family.

She paused as though she could still view the scene. "We had a lot of good times here."

Once in a while, said Vonda, an old-timer will come by with his grandchildren to show them what it was like when he was a kid. But more than not these days, Wabasis Lake is host to the same progressive creature comforts that define other inland lakes these days: Four-season castles ... high-falutin' bass boats .... motorized personal watercraft of every variety and horsepower ....

"We've just always rented rowboats, and without motors," said Vonda, noting that the price is now $10 a day, still reasonable, considering.

"Some of the guys bring their own motors now, but we only allow the small electric kind." She shakes her head. "Too much liability."

Her son, Patrick, has not moved from his spot in an easy chair in the home that overlooks Ace's Landing. He has been staring out onto the lake since I walked in.

He still fishes Wabasis a lot, but it's been a long time since Ace was at his side, the two of them bobbing about in a boat with oars as their only means of propulsion, and fishing with nothing more sophisticated than worms and cane poles.

"When I'm out there," he says, still staring, "it's relaxing. I don't think about a thing. Well, sometimes I do think about Grandpa," and Patrick says that he still hears Ace's favorite line echoing on the air, his response to the proposition that there might be grass to mow or a picnic table to mend. "Aw," Ace would tell his grandson, two poles in his hand, "we'll do it tomorrow."

If a man named Ace Wisinski could come back to visit Wabasis today, he might be stunned at the development, the noise, the summertime commotion.

But he'd be pleased that a grandson – and handful of others – still fish the old-fashioned way, and that his boats are still rented out, and that the slightest impression those oars make is when they dip and pull against the lake, creating those beautiful little crescents on the surface of the water that no motor could ever render.

Beauty of 'The Ridge' so Vivid in Fall

You can lay down a lot of miles in your romantic pursuit of autumn.

But it looms as large as anywhere along a windblown outcropping they call "The Ridge," where fruit growers and farmers have been honoring the harvest with a reverence passed down through the ages.

Like so many other things of beauty, it is anchored in paradox, as much an agrarian challenge as it is a picture postcard. Ask a man in John Deere green to extol it like a poem, and he just might chuckle, throw his tractor into gear and leave you wondering.

"Hell and heaven both," said Lenis Klein, 74, sporting two plastic knees and a bad ticker. "If it ain't hail, it's somethin' else."

To the passerby, The Ridge is an unfinished sculpture of rolling hills flush with orchards and pastures. Its skies are a thin skin of caramel plumes, and roadside markets are painted against hearty stands of crimson and gold.

But behind every bushel are people pulsing in a quiet rhythm to the change of seasons, squeezing daylight and time from both sides of the equinox.

"We just love to take a ride and look at the apples and all the color on the trees," said Joan Drake of Conklin, after buying fresh cider from the Klein & Sons mill on 10 Mile Road NW. "It's just so pretty."

That it is, this verdant spine of land that rises along the western edge of northern Kent County, hugging M-37 as it stretches between Int. 96 and the town of Casnovia.

Just ask Rosemary Arends.

"It doesn't get any better than this," she said. "Look at that view," and she casts her hand over the largest parcel of land in Sparta Township, north across 13 Mile Road NW from Steffens Orchard.

"Fresh air, space, wildlife, and some of the most excellent farmland in the state of Michigan," said Arends, who's in her early 70s.

This is a land of snapshots, taken along a continuum of families who have lived and worked here for well over a century.

"My kids are fifth-generation," said Jessica Curtis, 31, of her kids Victoria, 10, and Aaron, 2.

She tried living in Washington state after marrying her first husband. But it didn't work, and The Ridge kept whispering.

She moved back, married a man from Rockford, and they're staying put. "It has a lot to do with community," she said.

At the Klein place, Lenis' wife Dorace has just finished picking produce from a field thick with mud; her pantlegs are slick with it, but her yield rests in the bed of a red truck. Pretty soon, she'll head inside to make burgers and sweet corn for her boys.

That includes son Steve, 45, who still is smiling about the batch of special-needs school kids who just toured their 80 acres. One boy told his classmates, "That cow mooed at me."

For every joy on The Ridge, though, there seem counterpoints: A decent harvest, but too much time to make it happen. Some profit, but only if the government backs off migrant workers. So much land, but developers lurking behind every gravity box.

John Fryear is 41 and has never been married.

He sits atop a 2150 Case International, only mulling the future because he's been asked.

The past has been painful enough. Lost his dad at 16, and his mother Loretta is widowed twice now, most recently this past April.

She's sorting through wooden crates of Empires. Off her left shoulder, about 1,000 tomato plants still rage against pending frosts.

Fryear will inherit 80 acres, but it remains a question who might enjoy it after him, of what it might become.

You don't absorb loss, though, when you're just passing through, and plunk down your six bucks for a bushel of seconds to make applesauce.

Just thinking about her second husband prompts tears. Loretta never imagined herself alone against so many tomorrows.

That's the essence of living on the land, of living on The Ridge, of living anywhere worth living.

Says Loretta, turning another apple in her weathered hands, "You don't take much for granted."

Family's Story Told on One Farm Over 100 Years

Some of us see farms in a fleeting way, from speeding cars that only let us capture silobarnfield ... silobarnfield ... .

For Tom Moelker, though, it's a long slow movie 100 years in the making, most of it filmed in black and white, featuring a cast of characters that include a grandfather he never met and a father gone too soon.

"When I was young, I never really paid it a lot of attention," said Tom, the third generation of Moelkers to work the place. "I was just another kid on the farm."

Asked if he would do it over again – take the reins of 78 acres along the Grand River that for all of his 47 years has defined him – and he mulls the question a long time.

He thinks both about the bad crops that have beaten him down, and abundance that has propped up his family – not to mention nature's forces on the dozens of relatives that preceded him and his.

There have been workdays seemingly without end. Seasons without mercy. And years like 1986 when, at the age of 25, he not only lost his father, but had to finish the harvest largely on his own in one of the rainiest autumns on record.

"Do it over again?" he asked. "I don't know if I can answer that. But looking back, I can see God's hand in why I'm still in it.

"I'm here. And I guess there's a reason."

Perhaps it's so he and wife Bonnie, 44, and their kids, Travis, 14, Tressa, 12, and Taylor, 9, can stand back a few months from now and admire the green and yellow sign on order that will tell the world how Moelker Orchards & Farm Market is a Michigan Centennial Farm. Statewide, about 6,000 farms enjoy that status.

The Moelkers already have begun to celebrate. On Saturday, they will host a petting zoo. On that day and on Oct. 20, you're invited for cake.

Still, there's no way to fully communicate the vastness of 100 years, no single snapshot to suffice as history. And there are those who beg to know the future. Will son Travis step in to stay the family course? "Hard to say," Tom said. "We'd like him to go to college. After that, well ..."

In some ways, this spread on the Kent-Ottawa County line has changed in ways that would bewilder founder and Tom's grandfather, John Moelker.

Inside the farm market at 0-9265 Kenowa Avenue, you can buy apples and cider, sure. But there are modern-day articles as well – island punch candy sticks and Koko Krazy Kokonut Kandles.

Hubrecht Moelker was the first Moelker to settle here, directly from The

Netherlands. Son John and his wife, Elizabeth, helped Hubrecht run a small dairy farm in Southeast Grand Rapids before moving west to establish the farm on Kenowa in 1907.

John and Elizabeth, who had 10 children, were formally awarded the deed a year later, which explains why the state of Michigan won't hand over the centennial status until 1908. But nobody's holding a grudge.

John and Elizabeth bequeathed the place to Tom's dad, Jim, who died of cancer at 62. He married Donna, who survives, and they had four kids besides Tom, including two brothers who just didn't have the heart for farming. No grudges there, either.

It's pretty here today, with the sun climbing slowly to cast shadows from strands of dying vines that cling to the weathered barn. But there's work to compete with the poetry.

"Tough these days to sustain it just as a farm," Tom said. "But it's fun on a Saturday to see all the people goin' out of here smilin' with a bag full of apples. And to sit back at the end of the day and know all the fun they had."

His own smile fades some when you reckon how long it might be before developers work their own brand of magic.

"Really tempting, sometimes," said Tom, who will accept business cards but makes no promises.

He knows that farmland is dwindling. Statewide, more than 300,000 acres were lost to other enterprises between 1997 and 2002, according to the latest data available from the Michigan Department of Agriculture.

During the same period, in Kent County alone there was a 12 percent loss of farmland. The figures are less dramatic for Ottawa County, but still part of a trend.

"A pretty rapid dropoff," said Rich Harlow, MDA's program manager for farmland preservation.

When Hubrecht Moelker arrived here in 1888, half of all Michiganders lived on farms. Today, that number is 2 percent.

Even with a slowdown in building, farms such as Tom and Bonnie's – which includes a border along the Grand River – can be profitable if sold for development.

"But there's more to life than that," Tom said. "This is a neat place to grow up. My kids are probably the only ones in their schools from a farm. So I've never really given developers a reason to draft us a plan."

Sometimes, Tom and Bonnie stand on the river's edge, and they gaze out and wonder about all their ancestors who might have stood here before them, contemplating their own destinies.

Then it's Tom's voice again, echoing sounds of the past, and prompting more images of men and women who have come and gone. Maybe they're milking cows or discing a field or splitting maple. Maybe they're sipping lemonade amid lowing at sunset.

"And here I am," said a humble Tom Moelker, with a little laugh that asks as much as it tells. "Me still standing on this same piece of dirt."

Last Time Leaves Lasting Memory

In response to everyone who asked, "How were your holidays?," let me just admit now that I lied.

Or maybe that my answer was incomplete.

You know how it goes, of course. Someone wonders how your weekend was or how the vacation went, and you say, "We had a great time" or "It was super" or "Terrific."

When all the while, what you really want to share, at least in my case, is how "I tied my youngest boy's necktie for the last time."

We rarely mark the last time we do anything. We're more apt to record – either in a mental journal or a desktop diary – our inaugural milestones. They are easier to remember, easier to discuss.

There's the first time you went to Cedar Point.

The first time you volunteered at the pantry.

The first time you kissed someone, drove a car, ate a rutabaga or baled hay.

But how often have we been observant – or lucky enough – to recognize the last time we carried a child up the stairs to bed? Or ran a mile in less than six or seven minutes?

Will I be mentally savvy when the times come that I last make ice cream, drain one from half-court, buy flowers for my wife?

Teaching your son how to tie his tie is not a Richter-scale event. But strung together as part of everything a dad bequeaths to his sons, I like to think of it as significant.

A father's legacy is only as strong as what he leaves behind in word and example. And standing behind my boy with a mirror in the foreground is a moment so rich with metaphor and symbolism that, in the right hands, it could probably launch a novella.

In my instance, I was working a knot for our son, Andrew, a coming-of-age ritual that I performed and helped perfect for his older brothers, Tom and Patrick.

Our youngest doesn't need a lot of over-coaching.

He has the eye-hand thing down pretty well. So, going in, I knew it wouldn't be more than two or three times, and he would have the four-in-hand knot down.

Midway through our exercise, my hands slid atop his shoulders as I watched him arrange the two ends of the tie proportionately, then start the series of loops and folds that helps transform boys into young men.

In that moment, I saw my late father in the mirror, felt his knowing hands on my shoulders when I was 10 or 12. I yearned to feel like that just once more, and it simultaneously occurred to me that today might be the last time I stood with any of my sons like this.

My expression must have changed as my nostalgia gave way to gentle regret, because my kid asked "What's wrong?"

There was nothing wrong, just something ending.

And I tried to tell him, tripping over an explanation I didn't think he would be able to comprehend.

He did, though.

"That's OK, Dad," I heard, as he smoothed out a little dent in the fabric.

"You know, I could always forget."

How to Play Host for a Superstar

When Gordon Thayer tells the story about the woman he and his family entertained at their Algoma Township home, the response is always the same: "NO WAY!"

On the contrary. Way.

For it's true – that when country music sensation Shania Twain appeared in downtown Grand Rapids for her sold-out concert at the Van Andel Arena, she and her crew bunked at the Thayers' home, just a couple miles north of Rockford.

It's a well-kept secret that could only be told after her appearance here during the summer of 1998 – a condition the Thayers abided by out of respect for the internationally acclaimed performer.

"I was told afterward that of all the places she'd stayed during that tour, she had one of her best experiences here," says Thayer, who with wife Kathy owns a 20-acre horse farm on 12 Mile Road NE, just west of U.S. 131.

Horses, in fact, are a big part of the reason Shania chose the Thayer digs, because she insisted on touring that summer with her white Arabian in tow.

But hosting the famous singer might never have happened, had Gordon not severely injured his spine when he was a boy of 15 or 16.

During an 11-month rehabilitation at an area hospital, he spent long hours at the guitar. The practice paid off, and he has played professional gigs ever since, most recently as head of The Gordon Thayer Band.

He never lost his penchant for horses, either, and splits his time between playing a six-string and hosting riding camps for kids at the spread on 12 Mile, called "Happy Trails Stable."

Through a friend of a friend – he declines to be more specific – Gordon received a call two summers ago asking if he and Kathy and their two kids, Jesse, 12, and Kristina, 7, would play host to Shania.

"They told us up front that we couldn't discuss music with her, and that there would be no visitors," Gordon recalls.

They agreed, and under super-secret conditions, Shania and her horse and a crew of a half-dozen rolled in to absolutely no fanfare.

The Thayers didn't tell a soul. Not parents. Not siblings. Not Gordon's fellow band members. "I think that to this day, my next-door neighbor still doesn't know," says Gordon.

During Shania's two-day stay, the Thayers treated her as ordinary folk.

Gordon says it wasn't difficult to remain grounded in her presence. After all, in another lifetime, he himself played on stage with the likes of Rod Stewart, Jeff Beck and ZZ Top. And he lived in the same Bay City house for a year with the band that would later become known as Grand Funk Railroad.

The Thayers left Shania alone most the time, but did join her for one outdoor cookout, as well as a romp on horseback across more than 200 acres of open land that Gordon leased.

At one point, Shania – dressed in English riding gear – galloped off ahead of Gordon and a security person. Gordon thought nothing of it, until the other man exclaimed, "We can't let Shania go off by herself!" – and gave chase.

Other than that, it was a pretty calm 48 or so hours, save for the concert itself, to which the Thayers had VIP passes and backstage credentials.

After the show, the Thayers posed for photos with their guest, but never received a print, despite repeated appeals to her publicity staff.

Gordon says now that "I kick myself" for not asking Shania to autograph one of his eight guitars.

To say thanks for the hospitality, Shania sent the Thayers flowers and a pair of scuffed-up cowgirl boots, ostensibly hers.

For further proof of her visit, though, all the Thayers have is two or three minutes of low-quality video shot at the farm, which I viewed.

Shania looks as good dressed down as she does gussied up, an assessment Gordon agreed with.

Something else you notice when she is not in the limelight: Shorter hair. "No doubt she wears a hairpiece," says Gordon.

One other note of interest: The entire time Shania was at the ranch, no one on her crew ever addressed Shania as "Shania."

Her name is Eileen.

New Version of Carol Loses Something

When I attended St. James Catholic grade school during the 1960s, we'd be herded into the auditorium at the lunch hour with all our classmates – and be expected to remain silent the entire time we ate.

I always viewed that edict as bordering on barbaric. Being commanded to shut up during mealtime seemed like cruel and unusual punishment, especially for kids who already were expected to master the diagramming of sentences.

There was only one time during the year when my classmates and I were able to take sweet revenge –at the annual Christmas sing-alongs and pageants.

Specifically, it was the moment on stage when we got to sing the words to "Little Drummer Boy," one line in particular. And it was this:

"The ox and ass kept time, pa rum pum pum pum..."

Nothing cracked us up more at Christmas than the opportunity to sing the word "ass" while looking directly at our tight-lipped nuns. And in the many years since graduating from the eighth grade, I still take delight in singing those words every time I hear the tune.

But something weird has happened to "Little Drummer Boy" since it was first penned by the late Katherine K. Davis in 1941. People who resent the word ass as a synonym for donkey have begun singing "The ox and lamb kept time..."

I have nothing against baby sheep. But it doesn't have the same effect on music teachers and adults in a kid's midst as the word "ass."

If you use "lamb" as slang, it takes on soft, cuddly connotation.

"Ass," meanwhile, conjures up images of something altogether, as well as serving as a terrific prefix for all sorts of words that you won't find in a Catholic school dictionary.

In the last week or so, I've taken an informal poll of what people believe the line in the song to be. Most answer with the phrase "ox and lamb," but a smaller handful remember "ass" as the operative word.

During a search of Web sites, "lamb" outscored "ass" about four to one, with one set of lyrics displaying the line like this: "The ox and ass [lamb] kept time..."

Another really threw me for a loop by completely ignoring the ox and going with "The ass and lamb..."

The longer I thought about "ass vs. lamb," the more I wanted to know if, in fact, Katherine K. Davis did indeed pen "ass" rather than a more genteel animal. My search took me by phone and e-mail to the campus of Wellesley College in Massachusetts.

That's where Davis attended after graduating from high school in 1910. She planned to major in literature, but ended up earning a degree in music, then stayed on at the college to teach theory and piano. In her life, she composed more than 600 works before dying in 1980 at the age of 88.

Her most famous composition – co-authored with Harry Simeone and Henry Onorati – was "Little Drummer Boy," though it was first entitled "The Carol of the Drum." The lyrics, she is quoted as saying, came to her while trying to take a nap.

I tracked down Wilma R. Straight, who works in the archives of the Margaret Clapp Library at Wellesley, and she consulted a second source at the library, who tracked down the original manuscript which is safeguarded in the Wellesley College Music Library.

Katherine K. Davis, it turns out, was not one to mince words.

It's "ass."

Baseball Diamond Holds
Treasure Chest of Memories

I've run the Boston Marathon and bicycled the Canadian Rockies and backpacked wild Idaho and even parachuted – from my first ride ever in an airplane.

But as far as thrills go, I've batted .000 my entire life when it comes to Sullivan Field – formerly Valley Field – where I would give almost anything to play just one sun-drenched inning.

I came as close as I probably ever will just days ago, though, in ushering one of our own boys onto the isle of green to play in a fall-ball league with other 15- and 16-year-olds.

"You're playing on hallowed ground," I told him, and he nodded, acknowledging stories I'd shared of how his late grandfather – my dad – took to the same field in 1938, for a game deciding the Catholic grade school championship just one year after the field opened.

"I know," he answered, and in the next moment, was taking his place in center field, which backed up to the yard and adjoining home where my father's mother – my grandmother – spent her final years.

Her cupcake of a house on Fourth Street NW was a perfect spot to take in a game, and I never thought it a chore to paint her kitchen a canary yellow, what with honest hardball being played just across the chain link fence that enclosed the field alongside Valley Avenue.

Her house is still there, and I knocked on the door this past Friday, standing on the porch for the first time in more than 35 years. A yawning shirtless man answered it and said that no – from the backyard where Grandma hung her laundry and we drank lemonade with homemade molasses cookies – no, he watched no ball.

I asked, "Is the kitchen here still yellow?"

"Wallpaper," he said, and politely closed the door.

I am not the only one to rhapsodize about what many still call Valley Field – out of habit and no disrespect to Bob Sullivan, after whom the field is now named.

Ask almost anyone born and/or raised on the city's West Side, and you'll likely hear a sigh followed by talk of "wooden bleachers" and an umpire named John Blok whose claim to fame was raising two Vs of fingers and crooning, "Twooooooooooooo-twooooooooooooo!"

Old-timers still chat about teams spawned from blue-collar concerns like Grand Rapids Varnish and Dutch Kraft Paints and American Seating, factory nines whose ghosts still roam this sea of green tucked so beautifully into the working-class neighborhood where I grew up.

The faded grandstands hold 2,500, although in 1959 about 6,000 showed up to watch a youngster named Al Kaline pitch a victory for Sullivans over a collection of major league stars that included Jim Rivera, Sherm Lollar and Bob Shaw of the pennant-winning Chicago White Sox.

Tom Hoffman has a unique perspective on Valley Field, for he played on it, coached players there while at the helm of Grand Rapids Junior College and even worked the grounds while attending Catholic Central High School.

"Valley Field was it," he said, nodding to subordinates like Rumsey Park on Godfrey Avenue SW, where a dinger to right often resulted in another broken window at McInerney Spring & Wire Co. across the street.

"Valley was different because it had the seating, the stadium," he said. "It was a real ballpark.

"And it never let you down."

Fewer teams play there now, the dual effect of less interest in City Majors baseball and budget cuts that forced a padlock on the sprawling cathedral during the summer of 2006.

It's getting more action this year, thanks to an influx of area teams of teens hungry for summertime and autumn play.

"We've been doing a lot of work to get it back to what it used to be," said the groundskeeper there, Jerry Toogood.

On the day our son Andrew played, he caught the first out and later managed a clean hit between third and short. Everyone there assumed it landed in shallow left, but I know better.

That ball crossed the same base path his grandfather ran nearly 70 years ago, got tied up and then unfurled in a clothesline, hovered over a jug of lemonade and ascended into a sunny kitchen.

It's soaring still.

Aw Heck, Heaving Bales of Hay Takes Skill

There's something especially pastoral about farms. Photographers like snapping them. Painters relish capturing them with their palettes. And writers enjoy waxing poetic about the agrarian life.

But when you take away the big red buildings and silver silos and put your microscope on farms, there are few things as sweaty, as monotonous, as laborious – as heaving bales of hay.

It's what you'd discover if you went to a place like Max and Linda Dunneback's 75-acre dairy farm near Sparta. They put up a few thousand bales every year, and few people handle a bale like Max Dunneback.

The first time I saw him heave one, I thought, "How can a guy do that while balancing a little baby in each arm?" But those weren't babies. Those were his biceps.

Max stands 5 feet, 10 inches and weighs, in his words, "120 in dog pounds." But every ounce is dedicated to hard work – the only way things get done on a family spread that includes his wife and three children.

That work includes putting up bales of hay, and every year, Max showcases his know-how at Sparta's annual Town & Country Days celebration, which concludes today. Not only is he coordinator of the annual Bale Tossing Competition, but a former champ. What's more, his sister, Ginny Brown, is the women's defending medalist.

"Aw, you just grab it and give it a toss," says Max, who floored me with his rural prowess in chucking a bale about 32 feet during a practice session on his farm. "I think my best is 43," he muses, and that includes the roll, which can tack on several yards to the average toss.

For the past 12 years, first place in the Sparta competition has rocked back and forth between Max and Mark Vanderhyde. Although the names Luke Skrabis and Chad Momber also surface from year to year.

Last Saturday, however, a youngster – Mark Vanderhyde's 19-year-old son, Matt – bested all comers (his father was unable to compete) with a monstrous fling of nearly 41 feet. Matt, like his father, throws bales like a discus thrower, with a wind-up that culminates in the hay going airborne.

Matt wasn't the only winner last weekend. His younger brother, Kyle, 14, won the junior division. Tom Dunneback won the first-ever handicapped class, and 8-year-old Matt Slabbekoorn took blue ribbon honors for kids under 14. No women competed.

As for Max Dunneback, he finished a close second in the men's division, with a toss of 37 feet, 9 inches.

You might wonder what a desk jockey like me might do when armed with a bale. I wondered. So I entered, too. I sailed it just over 25 feet, good for sixth among 10 men competing. Which was a little better than the 15 feet or so I threw in practice on Max's farm a few days earlier.

Max fished an orange ribbon out of a plastic tub and declared me a bona fide country boy.

It was high praise. All the same, I'm keeping my city job.

You do that when you're afraid of cows.

Recipe for Romance

What would you do if a stranger knocked at the front door and asked to borrow your dining room for an hour?

Nancy Heiser said yes.

In doing so, she not only helped nurture the relationship between a young couple, but showed the rest of us the world is ruled as much by trust as it is risk.

Jacob Blakeney is a 21-year-old senior at Cornerstone University. He struggles to meet the expenses of college, so he did not have a lot of money to treat his girlfriend, Cornerstone sophomore Heidi LaBurn, also 21, on Valentine's Day.

He had remembered, though, that whenever he and Heidi traveled through East Grand Rapids on their way to Eastown, she would ask him to cruise past Lake Drive and Bonnell Avenue SE.

That is where she would breathe in the essence of the Heiser home, an exquisite country-French dwelling whose exterior boasts handmade bricks, a carved mahogany door and more than an acre of manicured grounds.

"She loves that home," Jacob says. "Every time we drive by, she makes me slow down."

Neither Jacob nor Heidi knew who lived there. But the week before Valentine's Day, he mustered the courage to drive there alone and beg a favor from whomever might answer the door.

It was Nancy – who with husband John, a heart surgeon everyone knows as Chuck – built the 8,000-square-foot palace 10 years ago.

Jacob introduced himself, explained how his girlfriend romanticized about the home, then asked Nancy if he could borrow their dining room to serve Heidi a Valentine's Day dinner.

"It was a rather bizarre request," Nancy allows. "But he presented himself well, and it was obvious that he'd thought this out.

"I was very touched by the whole thing. I mean, he had no idea who was behind the front door. But he was willing to do this for his girlfriend."

So she made an answer the rest of us might not have been so willing to give: Surely.

Jacob shared his phone number, then arranged to bring a pre-cooked meal to the Heiser home the afternoon of Valentine's Day. He'd arrive later in the evening with an unaware Heidi.

On the day of reckoning, Jacob cooked up Heidi's dinner in a crockpot – roast beef, potatoes and carrots. He snagged a bottle of sparkling grape juice, then drove to the Heiser home at 2727 Bonnell Ave. SE.

Nancy, too, had been busy. She took the time to remove leaves from the table, which is usually set for eight, to give the room a more intimate appearance.

She ordered a floral centerpiece from Ginko Studios at 951 Cherry St. SE, where lead designer J.D. Nixon was so touched by the circumstances, he arranged red roses and tulips in a ruby glass compote that was "especially romantic."

Finally, Nancy set the table with her finest – Irish Waterford crystal, and Classic Edition china from Lenox.

Jacob showed up as planned with the crock pot, then headed back for Heidi.

He made her close her eyes and slump down in the seat of his pickup, then drove in circuitous fashion to help throw off Heidi's sense of direction.

When they arrived on Bonnell, he told her to open her eyes.

"What are we doing here?" she asked.

"We're here for dinner," he answered.

"Are you serious?"

"Yes."

While they dined on stew in the glow of two red candles, which Nancy also had supplied, Nancy and her four children – John, 18, Evan, 15, David, 14, and Susan, 12 – retreated to the basement for their own Valentine's Day dinner of cheese fondue. Husband Chuck would have been there, but he was called to the hospital.

Before Jacob and Heidi left, Nancy appeared in the dining room to share the family's dessert – a "red velvet" cake.

Heidi later said she was caught breathless by her boyfriend's plan. "The fact that he went out of his way to do something like this is so special."

"I knew," Jacob says, "that she would appreciate it."

What he also knows is the catalyst for a romantic evening wasn't to be found in a stuffed teddy bear, a box of chocolates, a throwaway greeting card.

It revealed itself through the generosity of a woman who is trusting, who is kind, and perhaps most importantly, who understands affairs of the heart.

CHAPTER 5

Loss

Sad Farewell to Loyal Friend

My friend John now lives outside the area this newspaper typically circulates.

But years back, when he lived in Grand Rapids on Tenth Street NW, he had a dog named Candy.

I'd never had a dog, and I considered her as much a nuisance as I did someone's pet. When she got sick and had to be put down, John told me how he drove to Grand Haven one evening and walked to the end of the pier there. Together, they'd haunted that spot often.

I remember him telling me that after spending some time mulling over his loss, he ceremoniously pitched Candy's leash and collar into the beckoning waves. Wept, probably.

I didn't cry. Frankly, I couldn't empathize with anyone who ever had lost a pet. Dog. Cat. Parakeet. What was the difference? They were just a step above inanimate objects. Old Yeller was sad, but c'mon.

I found out yesterday, when I hauled our old dog Bear down the road for the last time.

A beautiful Golden Retriever, I'd brought her home as a surprise to Hollie, my bride of three months, when the downy pup was just six weeks old. That was nearly 12 years ago.

In all that time, she loved unconditionally. She was infinitely loyal. And not once did she interfere with the subsequent raising of our three sons, whom she guarded as her own.

Bear had a history even as I acquired her. It was my understanding that the gentleman to whom she had been sold detected problems with her eyes. So he received a refund from the breeder.

"You'd love this dog," the breeder, a friend of mine, told me. And he said we could have Bear for free, since the surgery to repair her eyes would cost about the same as a fair purchase price.

Like I said, I had never had a dog, not until 1987, when I was 33. But I can say now that no words could convey how much I cherished her. And Hollie's sentiments are even more acute; nearly every day, Bear used to accompany her on 5-mile runs. She was a constant companion.

One of Hollie's favorite snapshots is a rear-view of Bear and me heading out in my old pickup. And I do mean old. We looked like an Okie and his furry sidekick tooling down the road looking to score out odd jobs.

The dog was not overly gifted. My fault, I'm sure. Never trained her to do tricks with a Frisbee. Didn't get her into hunting. She swam all right, but would always try to clamber up on me, scraping my legs with her paws.

Do I miss that now.

This past Sunday at the beach, she fell while bolting after another dog, and yelped in response to a leg she'd already been favoring the last couple weeks.

We carried her 500 yards in a makeshift stretcher fashioned from a hammock. Her front left leg was useless.

A trip to the vet confirmed bad news: cancer. It was in her leg, shoulder and lungs. Give her a month, maybe, they said. You could make the decision now, but might feel better about putting it off some.

We brought her home, a sudden invalid. She'd never walk on that leg again.

I hearkened back to fantastic tales I'd read of amputee dogs, dogs in braces, dogs on gurneys.

Not my dog.

I didn't want her to spend her remaining days on her side. Dealing with pain and pain medications, never knowing for sure what effect they were having. And maybe worst of all, depending on me to lift her 80 pounds outdoors and up and down stairs every time she needed relief.

Last night, I called my wife and our three boys together. Family meeting, I announced. We met on one of the boy's bottom bunk beds.

We usually talk at family meetings. This time, we all just cried.

Yesterday afternoon, each son she had guarded hugged and kissed his dog goodbye. We talked about dog heaven and saying hello on our behalf to people who have passed. The image of my wife, weeping miserably as I started off with Bear in that same rusty truck, broke my heart.

The vet's hands were sure, his manner soft. "Ten seconds, and she'll be asleep." Then the real medicine would do its thing.

I cradled Bear's soft head in my hands, wept myself, and told her everything you might shout into the darkness from some pier.

Now, I understand.

'Skylee Taught Us How to Love Again'

Most parents never face the ultimate test.

But this noon, Terry and Valerie Sikma buried their second angel in seven years. And in the midst of their grief and wondering how and why, the Allendale couple are quietly teaching the rest of us what it means to love again. To touch and to hold and to believe.

In 1993, their son, Terry Lee – nicknamed T.J. – died of brain cancer at age 4. On Sunday, the couple's daughter, Skylee Starr, died from the effects of brain tumors. She, too, was 4.

Doctors have told the Sikmas that their children's deaths do not appear to be the result of a genetic defect. Just million-to-one odds devastating the same family twice.

Last night, hundreds of mourners – including Skylee's two older sisters, Tara and Jennifer – filed past a small white casket, saying tearful goodbyes to a little girl with golden curls wearing a pink dress festooned with butterflies. She cradled a stuffed dog in her arms, and wore a necklace with charms that read "Little Angel" and "I Love Papa."

"When T.J. died, we turned cold," said Terry Sikma, 45, a self-employed excavator whose trucks still bear his youngest children's names.

"We couldn't love," said Valerie, 44. "But Skylee brought us back to Jesus. We realize now that God sent us two angels. And it was our job to raise them both.

"I'm not bitter. Skylee taught us how to love again. We wish we'd had her longer, but at least she was given to us."

At Matthysse-Kuiper Funeral Home in Allendale, Valerie clutched her daughter's "blankie" to her chest as she worked through tears to greet visitors and thank them for their prayers and support.

It was a painful revisiting of seven years ago, although the family hopes to soften the blow by accepting gifts in Skylee's memory to continue financing a children's play area in Allendale Township Park that bears T.J.'s name. Envelopes are available through the funeral home.

Friends and relatives who knew Kylee described her last night in echoes. "Bundle of joy." "Sweetheart." "So happy." "Beautiful."

"She brought more sunshine onto this Earth in her four years," said a grandfather, Roger Sikma, "than I might in my whole lifetime."

She had taken ballet and tap dance lessons. Made forts in the snow. Dressed as a bunny rabbit and princess at Halloween. Worked alongside her papa while he was out getting his nails dirty. And when her mother said, "Thank you, God, for giving me Skylee," she'd say back, "Thank you, God, for giving me my mommy."

"How much does Mommy love you?" Valerie would ask.

"Too much," Skylee would reply.

Skylee Starr derived her name from a combination of her late brother's middle name, Lee, and the shining star he symbolically occupied each time the Sikmas would raise their eyes to the night sky, searching for signs.

Valerie had had trouble conceiving T.J., and after he died, she underwent a reversal of her tubal ligation so that she might conceive again. She was given just a 30 percent chance, but in six weeks became pregnant.

"Skylee wasn't given us to replace T.J.," said Valerie, "but to fill Mom's arms again.

"She was my miracle."

Skylee was born healthy, and celebrated this past Christmas with gifts of a Barbie cash register and a Skateboard Shannon. Two days later, she was diagnosed with tumors in her brain stem.

She grew worse over the past few weeks. Terry would give her his trademark piggy-back ride to bed, then sometimes slumber alongside her. His wife would occupy a nearby couch.

On Sunday night, knowing the end was imminent, they brought their curly haired girl into their bed. Terry sat close while Valerie cradled Skylee's head in the crook of her left arm.

Neither parent knew whether Skylee might manage any last words that evening. But they would do their best to communicate with her until the end, and not in euphemisms, but real words a dying child might understand.

"Is Jesus talking to you?" Skylee's mom asked through tears.

Her baby nodded.

"Are you gonna go play with T.J. now?"

Another little nod.

She hugged her Skylee close.

"How much does Mommy love you?"

"Too much," whispered Skylee Starr, and she went to join her brother.

Painful Puzzle

Every morning would begin the same – with three crossword puzzles. He would take his place in the dark green La-Z-Boy, and she would sit on his lap. Together, they'd revel in a game of synonyms.

Their dream together ended abruptly, however, on Oct. 17 when Bill Boeskool died from injuries suffered in a one-car accident on westbound Int. 96 near the Dean Lake Road overpass.

Bill and his wife, Carolyn, had both been married before – Bill for 45 years and Carolyn for 41 – but both were widowed several years ago. Carolyn lost her husband in 1998 to a heart attack. Bill lost his wife the year before from complications after surgery.

A mutual friend lined them up on a blind date. Carolyn was living alone in Muskegon, and Bill agreed to meet her after visiting a friend there.

She remembers being nervous. But when Bill arrived, he asked her to tell him about her family.

"I could tell he was used to talking to people," Carolyn recalls.

They were married last January. He wore a dark blue suit, she wore a burgundy velvet dress. After exchanging vows, he read a limerick he wrote just for her.

Bill was well known in the Grand Rapids area not only as an actor, but as teacher, coach and counselor with East Grand Rapids Schools. Carolyn retired recently as an educator.

"There were some differences we had to iron out," Carolyn remembers. "We'd both lived different lives for so many years."

But the second marriage for both took off soaring. Bill liked to golf, so Carolyn went, and when she hit one into the woods, he would say something gracious like, "Well, you had a nice powerful swing there."

She was active in her church, and the week before the accident, Bill approached the pastor and asked how to become a member.

Every night at the dinner table, they'd join hands and pray for their kids, for their grandkids, for their world.

"Everything was melding," she remembers. "We were so happy, the two of us."

She was on an overnight trip when word came that Bill had lost control of his car and crashed into an embankment, sending the car end over end. She got back too late to hold or speak to him before he died, her groom of just 10 months.

A state trooper at the scene told the family that someone, possibly a doctor, had stopped to offer assistance to Bill immediately after the crash. It's believed that whoever stopped also prayed with Bill before he was taken to the hospital.

Carolyn lies awake at night wondering who the person was. What Bill said. The pain he endured. His last words.

It's not the sort of puzzle you figure out with a thesaurus.

Just the aching need of a woman who has lost two husbands in three years. Any clues?

Samaritans Offer Prayers, Final Comfort

In a column that appeared Sunday, I wrote of Carolyn Boeskool's desire to know more details surrounding the death of her husband, Bill, who died Oct. 17 in a one-car crash just outside Grand Rapids.

Bill and Carolyn – both widowed in recent years – were married only 10 months, and she was heartbroken not only for the short time they had spent together, but because she couldn't be there to comfort him in his last moments.

She specifically wondered about comments from a trooper at the scene who thought someone had prayed with Bill before he was transported to a hospital, where he later died.

Turns out it was true.

And then some.

Bill was a coach, counselor and educator for many years at East Grand Rapids Schools. Carolyn spent most of her career in education at Muskegon Schools.

They met on a blind date and married in January.

Carolyn was out of town overnight when word reached her that Bill had lost control of his car and it had flipped end-over-end along westbound Int. 96 near the Dean Lake Road overpass. He was thrown from the vehicle and suffered internal injuries, succumbing before Carolyn could return home.

The first person to e-mail me after the column ran was Lisa Caron, a 39-year-old self-employed accountant from Cedar Springs, who witnessed Bill being thrown from the vehicle after it struck a hard-packed embankment.

She stopped and was the first person to his side.

She said she had thought about contacting Bill's survivors as his funeral approached, and finally decided to do so after reading the column. She gave him the jacket off her back, then stayed with him until others arrived.

That included Shawn De Jonge – who also read the column and contacted me. He's a 31-year-old art teacher for Wyoming Public Schools.

Shawn and friend Rick Rusthoven were taking a short break from their Bible study group, and used the opportunity to test-drive Shawn's new 1995 Honda Odyssey.

They happened on the accident shortly after Lisa.

Shawn remembers Lisa's presence, along with that of a second woman, who used her cell phone to call 911. Shawn says Rick sat on the ground next to Bill and made sure he didn't move. Meanwhile, Shawn ran to Bill's car, perhaps 25 feet away, and ripped the carpet lining from the trunk.

The foursome used the lining – along with coats provided by both women now – to wrap Bill up and keep him warm.

Shawn recalls thinking initially that it wasn't that bad an accident.

His opinion changed, though, when he saw Bill, who appeared to be in shock and seemed unable for the most part to communicate.

Shawn and Rick "felt the need – the urgency – to pray for Bill." Carefully, they placed their hands on his shoulder and "prayed that the Lord comfort him and sustain his life and give him peace. We asked the Lord to take care of him."

Shawn, of course, shared his story with Carolyn Boeskool. So, too, did Lisa Caron.

She was heartened by what they did. "Nothing's going to bring Bill back," Carolyn told me after communicating with Shawn and Lisa, "but just knowing more about how he spent his final moments is a comfort to me."

Carolyn said she was especially struck by the giving nature of those who assisted her husband. "It's important to me to know that someone had prayed for him, that he wasn't alone, that the people who stopped were such gentle people, such Samaritans."

Shawn told me over the phone that he'd forgotten to share one more thing with Carolyn, and that's what he and Rick did after returning to their Bible group at a home in the Creston Heights area.

They joined eight others and meditated on a man en route to the hospital; a man who couldn't be joined by his wife, but in his final moments was cloaked in warmth, touched by strangers, delivered up on the wings of prayer.

'Greatest Person I Have Ever Known'

Teddy Knape lived for three things:
Fair winds.
Fresh powder.
And others.
So when they carried him off a British Columbia mountaintop this past Sunday, friends and family not only mourned the passing of a 21-year-old graduate from East Grand Rapids High School taken too soon, but celebrated the fact that he died doing what he loved.

He will be buried Friday in a pine casket adorned with more than a dozen skis that were lovingly affixed by family and friends Wednesday evening.

And his short story is one that every one of us should reflect upon, especially if we ever have faced down a dream and given in to laziness or apathy.

He worked uphill his whole life, beginning with a heart defect at birth that would stalk him to the last. Not that he used it as an excuse. Most who knew him were unaware of his history, said parents Bill and Cindy Knape.

Nor were most aware of his three heart surgeries, a blood disorder that demanded lifelong medication, a car accident that shattered his leg and jaw, and more than a dozen accidents that required stitches.

As a youngster self-conscious of the scars he sported, brothers Peter and Paul invented a story about how Teddy had fought off an alligator. The holes in his legs, they told other kids, were where he fired shots to kill the beast. The long, jagged scar on their brother's chest was where Teddy's flailing with a knife missed the critter.

In truth, though, Teddy Knape created his own drama, mostly with a video camera. When he wasn't attending college or working part-time for his father, who is president of Knape Industries in Algoma Township, he was winning regattas or filming daredevil skiers for a company based in the Pacific Northwest called Theory-3 Media.

It's what he was doing until the end, high atop peaks at Whistler ski resort in British Columbia, at an extreme-skiing event known as the K2 Back 9. A helicopter pilot ferrying the sport's top skiers for the filming saw him collapse.

One of Teddy's many friends called the Knape home in East Grand Rapids to report he was in bad shape, and shared a number for the clinic where he was taken.

Cindy, a registered nurse, called and connected to another RN who said, "We're doing all we can."

In the next moment, Bill spoke to a doctor who expressed every parent's worst nightmare: "I pronounced him five minutes ago."

Their rage and disbelief gave way to acceptance. Even with the heart problems, they thought their son would live to celebrate more decades. But let's mourn differently, they decided, a boy who sailed and skied not for recreation, but as a way of life.

"We're proud that we were able to let him live the life he wanted to live," said Cindy, "and not hold him back."

Teddy was the heir apparent to his father's business. But he never flaunted a life of privilege. He was clicking off classes toward an engineering degree at Western Washington University on Puget Sound, where he could study and enjoy the snow and water.

Before his graduation in 2003 from EGR High, he distinguished himself there in sailing, and by making the ski team as a freshman. His ailments forced him to quit, but without complaint. He just switched gears and began a love affair with filming skiers that blossomed into a solid job with Theory-3. The shots he performed put him ski-to-ski with professionals who heaped praise on him for his videography skills and his propensity to inspire others with his unbridled joy for living.

"When I have kids, and they are struggling in school or complaining about something trivial," professional skier Zach Davison wrote in tribute, "I will sit them down and I will tell them of my friend Teddy Knape, the greatest person I have ever known."

On a Web site dedicated to the skiing community, Cedric Tremblay-Fournier posted this note: "He's skiing with God now."

Last year, Teddy Knape endured his third heart surgery, and while recuperating, noticed his mother having her own medical problems. She was eventually diagnosed with multiple sclerosis. Teddy became her caregiver, and when Cindy would ask her son how he was feeling, he would answer, "No, Mom, how are you feeling?"

From that day forward, every time he signed off with her on the phone, it was with the words, "I love you Mom." The two spoke by phone a week ago, and those were his last words to her.

Bill will miss their special times together on the water. "We sailed together. He was the boss." Looking toward another season of wind, he swallows hard: "That'll be hard."

In recent days, Cindy has wondered what it would have been like to shelter her son more, and whether it would have been "easier if he was sitting on a couch and not skiing."

She looks up through the tears of a mother who knows better.

"That's not who he was."

Young Voices Prepare Songs of Thanks, Mourning

With Saturday's Christmas program behind them, an elite group of singers from Northview High School is training for a performance no one wanted to give, but none would consider missing.

They are practicing for the funeral of beloved school counselor Deana Novakoski, who, after battling ovarian cancer for seven years, has decided to forgo her feeding tube and is expected to die within days.

At Deana's request, Northview's Varsity Voices will help send off the 49-year-old educator known to friends for her devotion to others.

Even her final act – to disconnect the feeding tube – is viewed as a gift, in that to continue using it would only compound the care required before her death.

Deana spends her final days in a room of the home she shares with husband, Terry, in northern Kent County.

That's where I went Friday to visit her, a woman I've known since she was a young teen in a swim class I taught at Richmond Pool, not far from the West Side home where then-Deana Sweers and her six siblings grew up.

During the hour we talked, the only regret she allowed herself was she will not see daughter Emily, 24, have babies, or son Matt, 22, marry. Every other word from her parched mouth was of others.

A tear rolled slowly from her right eye as she extolled in ragged breaths a Northview "community" that she emphasized included everyone from the guys who sweep hallways to the office of the superintendent.

She talked, too, of dreams she wills herself to have, specifically of the outdoor pools where as a young woman she served as lifeguard.

"The most calming," she said, "are of being splashed in the face with water, snagging my suit on the concrete, and the warm sun on my face."

In preparing her last rites, Deana has fretted about those she will leave behind after 16 years at the school, relaying to Principal Mark Thomas her concern that students drive safely if making their way from the church to the cemetery.

"This whole process," said Thomas, "is the giving of a gift. All her professional life, she has been this beautifully astute, emotional caregiver. And it continues."

He took a tough breath of his own: "Even now, she's looking for the teachable moment."

A self-professed "planner" even unto her own end, Deana has had a hand in writing her obituary and selecting the songs and voices who will perform at St. Jude's Catholic Church.

The latter task has fallen to 24 juniors and seniors who auditioned to become part of the school's Varsity Voices. They're used to performing at other schools and nursing homes, for service clubs and private parties.

But for the counselor they've come to know and love?

"It's really going to be important for us to hold it in," senior Lauren Wernstrom said. "My first reaction was, 'I can't do this.' But if Mrs. Nova can go through all that she's gone through, how can I not give back?"

"So selfless," Lauren said of the woman who served as her counselor. "And loving," added Hannaniah Whitley, who will perform a solo during the upcoming Mass. "Courageous, too," said senior Dylan Mason.

In seven years, Deana endured countless operations, the last one running 18 hours and performed by two surgeons. It bought her time, but likely not enough to see another Christmas.

She enjoyed her last bit of real food this past February, and for 10 months has relied on nutrients delivered via a port in her chest. In recent weeks, though, her body has been unable to absorb even that, and in consulting with her doctor, made the decision Dec. 4 to stop feeding, to go with grace.

Her husband of 26 years stands vigil along with their two children and a host of extended family. Tough as it is to watch his wife die, Terry, 51, says, "We can't ask to change the master plan. Then you're trying to be God. And none of us can be that."

"They've seen me suffer for months," Deana says. "And I've encouraged them and convinced them that there's a better place for me. They'll see me again in a different realm. And I'll be around. They'll call me and I'll hear."

Deana's convinced, too, she'll be listening when the Varsity Voices congregate to sing "Seasons of Love," "Sing Me to Heaven" and "There is no Rose of Such Virtue."

Northview's vocal music director, Judy Pellerito, can't promise she won't break down as she conducts that day for the woman who has become a best friend. "We'll get through it," she says, "But I'm a crier."

Her singers will need to focus, she says. They're going to be gazing out into the pews and seeing "a lot of adults in their lives just crumbling, and those adults are going to be looking for us to help them express their grief, because that's what music does."

At least three people will speak at Deana's funeral, but cards and letters to the couple's home have already brought dozens of voices to Deana's bedside.

"You were always there for me," Tori VanDragt penned on pink stationery.

One teacher referred to Deana as the "glass half-full girl," and another, Sheridan Steelman, composed a poem in which she wrote, "Your kindness has always been our warm cocoon ... Now let our love carry you to your destiny."

Those sentiments and more will be imbued in a Mass that will include readings from the Bible and prayers whispered by family and friends.

In large part, though, it will fall on the shoulders of two dozen kids to sing perhaps like never before, digging deep for the poise required to lift those lyrics up to the skies, a fitting gift for the giver, songs in the key of Deana.

A Little Girl, Now an Orphan, Learns What it Means to Have A Family Forever

This is Molly Karen Markoski, age 2, and you may be meeting her here for the first time, though you have likely thought of her, grieved for her, prayed for her, even wept for her.

Like the child or grandchild you might fawn over later this evening, she is being put to bed with stories and prayers, under the watchful eye of Pooh, Tigger and other stuffed animals.

But this isn't Molly's mother at her side. It's not quite the same bedroom she grew to know during the first two years of her life. And the dreams she dreams are those of a youngster starting over, whether she knows it yet or not.

Molly is the blonde-haired, blue-eyed girl orphaned six and a half weeks ago when a speeding car slammed into her family's minivan on Int. 196 just west of the Lake Michigan Drive exit.

Her father Fred, 33, a supervisor at Brooks Beverage in Holland, was killed. Her mother Kris, 31, a respiratory therapist who recently quit to provide daycare in her home, was killed. Her younger brother Benjamin, 10 months, was killed. Both young men in the other car – John Hardin, 23, and Jason Walczewski, 22, who was drunk at the wheel – were killed.

Only Molly survived, spending 10 days hospitalized with breaks to her right arm and left leg.

Most of us came to know the horror of it through news reports. Molly's grandparents in Grand Rapids were notified by the late-hour arrival of three police officers and a Catholic priest stepping softly to their front door.

Other friends and relatives found out via phone calls, and they fell into each others' arms as they met at the hospital to say tearful goodbyes. And to help Molly go on.

She lives now in South Haven with her uncle Jim and aunt Karla VanderRoest. Karla, formerly Karla Kiry, is older sister to Molly's late mother, and godmother to Molly.

In the blink of an eye, Jim and Karla have gone from caring for one child – 11/2-year-old Nathan – to two. But they don't regard it a hardship.

"We always said we wanted two kids," says Jim, a senior research chemist for a South Haven firm. He smiles. "Or even three of four."

He and Karla, who recently quit teaching elementary school to serve as full-time mom, manage one day at a time. That includes this day, a holiday whose theme seems ironic in light of last month's tragedy.

Yet, Molly's new family is trying to be thankful. Despite the losses that made no sense that Sunday evening, they are grateful for the opportunity to help usher a little angel toward her own destiny.

"It might be kind of strong to say we're celebrating," Karla says. "But we're certainly getting together to acknowledge that life goes on."

After the Markoskis died, Jim and Karla, both 30 and wed in 1990, vowed to give Molly the kind of love and life her own parents would have provided. They seem to have spared nothing toward that end.

Shortly after it was agreed by relatives that they would serve as her guardians (no will was ever discovered) the VanderRoests gathered up Molly's bedroom furnishings from her home on Fourth Street NW in Grand Rapids and transplanted them in the same configuration at their South Haven address.

They changed the paint from off-white to white. They found the same wallpaper Molly had enjoyed before. And they decorated the walls with dolls and needlepoint Molly's mother had both bought and made. The room smells like fresh wash sunning on the line.

Photos of Molly's family look out at her from a bulletin board, and from other locations throughout the VanderRoest home. "We don't want Molly to ever forget them," says Karla, gazing out at Molly from a seat in their kitchen. "Whatever they did, they did with their children in mind."

The pictorial reminders are especially bittersweet for Karla. She and her sister – Molly's mother – were soulmates. They spoke long-distance almost every night, and Karla can hardly contain herself to remember.

She pockets her own grief, though, to attend to a little girl who knows all her Sesame Street characters, can count beyond 10, and loves back when kissed and hugged.

Molly's memory of the tragedy, which occurred while the Markoskis were returning from an Oct. 12 family gathering at the VanderRoest home, seems fleeting. On occasion, she will say, "Minivan go boom," and she recalls the presence of rescue personnel. A passing trucker used his pocketknife to cut her from her back-seat child restraint.

While recuperating in the hospital, Molly cried out often for her parents. Those requests have faded as Jim and Karla help her face the truth, which a child psychologist told the VanderRoests they are smart not to sugar-coat.

"She knows her mommy and daddy are gone," Karla says sadly, "and that we miss them, too."

Karla and Jim, who belong to Hope Reformed Church in South Haven, say they will help Molly more fully explore concepts like heaven when she is better able to process life and death.

For now, the VanderRoests know she might be remembering more than she expresses. "The other night," says Karla, "she was lying in bed singing 'Rock-a-bye, Molly, in the treetops . . . '

"She sang the whole way through, and neither one of us had taught her that one."

And a bubbly Molly will sometimes blurt out phrases like, "Whatcha' doin' there, Karla?," and "Momma silly, daddy funny," expressions she'd developed before the accident.

Karla's mother, Karen Kiry, believes support from family on both sides has helped her granddaughter cope. "She's probably doing better than all of us," she said.

It is easier to monitor Molly's physical progress. Her arm is cast-free, and a second cast now covering her left leg and hip should be off before Christmas. The morning I visited, she chowed down on FruitLoops and juice, sang songs to kids' cassette tapes, played with Jim's and Karla's visiting mothers, and waved to vehicles coming and going in the VanderRoest driveway.

"Beep, beep," said Molly, as cars honked their departure from her new family's home.

Karla says she and Jim admit to being "overwhelmed" at times to suddenly be caring for two. "But then I look at Molly's smiling face, and Nathan's smiling face, and it just makes everything a little better." They also bow to a crowd of supporters who hail from their church and elsewhere.

Karla and Jim are keeping a scrapbook for Molly. It includes scores of photos showing her with her first family, and with kin hailing from both sides.

Karla is saving mementoes as well, some for Molly and others for herself. Near Karla's own bed, she keeps a brown corduroy coat that belonged to her sister. She sometimes cradles it while remembering. She has a blue shirt of Benjamin's. "It smells like him. It smells like their house."

Others in the extended family continue to grieve as well. Fred Markoski's parents, Norbert, 72, and Glennis, 70, are haunted by what the accident scene must have been like. They try to focus elsewhere.

Glennis, who has multiple sclerosis and needs assistance walking, recalls that not long before the accident, she fell down twice while trying to make it from their West Side home to their car. Fred showed up to help, wrapping his arms about her and carrying her the distance.

Glennis says Fred joked afterward that "Mom, two hugs in one day is too much." Hardly.

Norbert remembers meeting the priest and officers at the door. How they broke the awful news. Since the accident, while in the company of surviving sons, he's erred and called out, "Freddy." His eyes well with tears.

Norbert and Glennis know today will be unlike any other Thanksgiving. Both families do.

Their strength, they agree, is in Our Lord, and in each other, and so the whole clan planned to gather today for a traditional dinner.

"The happy times," Norbert struggles to say. "The good times we've all had with Freddy and Kris and Benjamin. All you have to do is pick up a paper to see those who aren't as fortunate.

"We've still got Molly."

Linda Will Always Be an 11-Year-Old

It has been 10 years since we lost our blond-haired school crossing guard. She would have turned 21 this month, and perhaps be cheerleading for her college teams, still playing the clarinet, still friends with the same six girls. All young women now. *Twenty-one.*

Ten years since she walked out the front door tugging on her knapsack, smiled as her mother said, 'Bye-Bye Puppagenie, have a good day," answered with "See ya' later alligator," then skipped a few feet down the sidewalk, turned, and waved goodbye to the face in the picture window.

We grieve each time we think of Linda Vanderveen, stare at the picture of the little girl who so easily could have been our own, who never got to turn 21, or even 12. It was 1979, two days before Valentine's Day, one of Linda's favorite days, and we wept when they found the sixth-grader's body, nine hours later, strangled with her own necklace, in a snow bank.

There were immediate concerns that Linda had been murdered by someone bearing a grudge against her father, Andrew, then personnel director for the city of Grand Rapids. In the end, they convicted Albert Lee III and sentenced him to life. Andrew died four years ago of a heart attack. Linda's older brother, David, is married and living in Maryland.

Linda's mother, Shirley, still avoids the corner where it happened – Orville Street at Rosewood Avenue SE – yet talks of her child with unbreaking voice, acknowledging that time heals, but only if you have faith.

"You have to believe in God," Shirley says. "I think – no, I know – that you can get through anything if you have that."

Shirley has forgiven Albert Lee III, but she received letters from anguished parents who sustained a similar anguish and were never able to do the same with their child's killer. Some of those couples divorced, most remained intensely angry. "They were sad people," says Shirley. "I remember turning to my husband and saying, "That's not going to be us, is it?"

We talked for more than an hour inside her Southeast Side home, and she rose once from the couch to get Linda's photo. It is a color photo, and tucked within the frame's edges are five other photos, all of Linda's school friends. The photos show the friends not as they were at 11, but as they are today. It is a bittersweet portrait of the past and present.

Shirley says it seemed unusual when she and Andrew were first approached and asked to approve a festival commemorating Linda. They consented after it was suggested that out of tragedy, joy might spring. Shouldn't we celebrate the memories of Linda's life, the parents were asked, and surround ourselves with the power and impact one child imparted on so many? Share her, they implored.

The 10th annual festival was held Saturday at John Ball Park. The crowds remembered the Mulick Park Elementary School student through the simplicity and innocence of paper bag puppets, balloons, face painting and all that is childlike.

Shirley has been sharing Linda since the day she received Linda's six friends into the Vanderveen home. The nightmare was still fresh when they appeared on the front porch, and Shirley invited them in, but both parties felt so awkward at first.

Eventually, they climbed the stairs to Linda's room. "We all went in and sat on Linda's bed," Shirley remembers, "and they tried on her jewelry, and her clothes." At Shirley's gentle urging, the girls took some things of Linda's home with them. "That was part of the healing process for both them and me," says Shirley.

"They came back after that for months," Shirley says of Linda's friends. "I needed them and they needed me. I feel as though I was so blessed, to have them there then."

Shirley has immersed herself in volunteer work since shortly after Linda's death. She works at a counseling center, at her church, at a hospital. She also cares part-time for two older people. One is a 77-year-old woman who last year lost her 43-year-old daughter to multiple sclerosis.

Shirley and the woman shared each other's burdens: "It doesn't matter how old a child is," says Shirley. "She went through the same hurt I did, the same feelings I did. It was very difficult for that mother."

Several times a year, Shirley visits Woodlawn Cemetery. Every February for sure, the month Linda was killed. There is often snow on the ground. Twice now, Shirley has been surprised to find footprints leading from the road to Linda's grave.

It was very recently she discovered that the footprints in the snow belonged to one of her six special friends, who still makes a wintertime visit to the girl who stayed 11.

"I can look at older girls with long blond hair and think, 'That could have been Linda,'" says Shirley, "but that child never grows up in your mind."

That is how Shirley remembers her. Eleven. Still young enough to call her by a spontaneous nickname like "Puppagenie." And still alive in spirit, giving us all something bright, something shining. That is how we must all remember our little school crossing guard, from our own picture windows."

CHAPTER 6

Labels

Scroll Show Leaves Me Feeling Flat

Ladies and gentlemen – Jews and Gentiles – first things first.

They're not exactly the Dead Sea "Scrolls."

They're more like the Dead Sea "Tidbits" – teeny, tiny fragments of antiquated parchment that, without scholarly interpretation, most of us couldn't discern from the scribblings of preschoolers.

Interesting? Yes.

Important? Certainly.

But given a choice, I'd probably rather take in a decent gun and knife show.

Blasphemy?

Nope. It's just that the ongoing exhibit that's being hyped beyond comprehension at the Van Andel Museum Center in downtown Grand Rapids doesn't float my boat.

And frankly, I'm wondering if there's anyone else out there who was underwhelmed by this latest take on The Emperor's New Clothes.

I'm also a little disappointed to learn that from now on, when the museum says it's got a coup on something, I need to start digging for the asterisk.

While I suppose it's still accurate to say that these specific Dead Sea Tidbits aren't being displayed elsewhere in North America this year, there are other Dead Sea Tidbits to be featured soon in a Tennessee exhibit.

And while museum officials clearly knew this back in January, they did little or nothing to acknowledge the Tennessee venue until confronted recently by a reporter from this newspaper.

Their reaction was to pooh-pooh it away, citing the apples-and-oranges defense. But my daddy raised no dummy. A Tidbit is a Tidbit.

And it makes me wonder about the boasting and crowing behind other exhibits the museum's hosted since opening its doors.

The discovery of the Dead Sea Tidbits is one captivating story. And you can't argue their historical and spiritual significance.

But for something that cost well over $1 million to erect, I was expecting different.

I'm not going to complain about the $14 entry fee, although a part of me wonders if this is such a must-see, why not throw the doors open in exchange for a free-will offering? Something tells me that's what the authors of the Tidbits might have preferred.

For those of you who haven't viewed the Tidbits yet, allow me to set the stage.

It's poorly lit, and it includes architectural elements that terminate in mid-air. I didn't get it.

The Tidbits themselves are enclosed atop marble bases, but little (no pun intended) was done to make them stand out from other artifacts that make up the exhibit.

I was expecting velvet-roped corridors to a separate staging area, or something equally elaborate.

As you tour the area, individual headsets feed you information not only about the Tidbits, but an ancient people and their culture.

It might have been entertaining had the voices in my ears sounded less professorial.

Think World History class and some geezer in a tweed coat with pipe ashes caught in his beard.

The Tidbits were well-attended the morning I wandered, especially by groups of schoolchildren.

But don't tell me at least some of them – and their teachers – were less excited by the Tidbits themselves and more about blowing off a day in the classroom.

I almost forgot to tell you about the gift shop where you can buy Tidbits paraphernalia after viewing the exhibit. Fake urns containing fake Tidbits are all the rage, a clerk there told me.

I would have popped for a necktie there depicting the Tidbits, but the price was nearly 60 bucks. And, to tell you the truth, I'm saving up for a shiny new Remington.

Here's a New Honor System

I call 'em "chest thumpers."

They're the signs rimming cities big and small that boast of a town's heroes, that trumpet favorite sons and daughters.

Trouble is, nearly all of them hail the accomplishments of athletes. You know what I mean. You're driving into a town, and there it is, white letters on green: "Welcome to Bisdoodle, Home of 1987 Girls High School Basketball State Champs."

Or this: "Currierville: Boys Cross-Country Champions, 1990, '91, '92."

There's nothing wrong with this, or even troubling. It's great, heralding the prowess of a town as defined by its fastest, strongest, highest-jumping.

But there could be more, or different, types of signs.

There could be signs that honor the everyday heroes in our midst, the knock-kneed and the awkward and the uncoordinated who never excelled on the field, but made a difference in someone's life – without ever donning a track uniform or football helmet.

Just once, I'd like to crest a hill and see in triumphant letters something like "Franville. Mel VanOtten Lives Here. Gives Cut Flowers Away for Free."

Or this: Puddindale: Home of Althea Wilson, Who Still Kneads Bread By Hand."

Maybe towns could invest in a revolving sign of sorts, one that might pay homage to a different hometown hero from month to month or even week to week.

Folks who lived there could nominate from among their friends and relatives, and it would generate renewed interest in "neighboring," which is to know more than just what you can glimpse from the privacy of your backyard deck.

The concept of signs to honor Mr. And Mrs. Average so overcame me recently that I imagined taking a drive about West Michigan, encountering a string of signs like the ones below. ...

"Welcome to Cedar Springs, Where Boyd Newsome Gave Up Playing Cards to Coach Little League."

Howard City says "Howdy" to LaVerne Nettles, Who Still Darns Her Husband's Socks.

"Mancelona Salutes Andy Hiller – Age 94, And Still Tithing.

"Welcome to Kalkaska, Home of Jessica Timpson – Whitest Teeth This Side of Port Huron."

"Now Entering Trufant, Where Nettie Cadwell's Been Using The Same Kitchen Cabinets For 58 Years."

"Hoxeyville Tips Its Hat to Marti Nessen, Who Never Turned Away a Stray Animal."

"Big Rapids Is Big On Jeanette Drabble: Loves To Whistle."

"Onekama's Pride: Chuck Brubaker, Who Never Forgets A Birthday."

"Tustin Loves Glenn Forrester: He Never Brings His Work Home."

"Acme, Home of the Rev. Joe Malnor. Never Preaches More Than Six Minutes."

"Saugatuck Salutes Roy Purdy: He Never Hangs Up on a Telemarketer Without First Saying 'Have A Good One.'"

"Welcome to Paw Paw, the Home of Justin Rivers. Reads Three Books A Week."

"Orangeville City Limits. Wave Hello to Fred Whitley. Still Flies Old Glory Every Day."

"Allegan Salutes Jim Barnes. Never Owned A TV."

"Fennville Loves Vern Cushman. A 10th-Grade Dropout Who Keeps Everyone's Car Running."

"Now Entering Beulah, Home of Uncle Bud, Who Never Asks His Nephews To 'Pull My Finger.'"

"Suttons Bay. Just Trying To Be Good People."

"Welcome to Falmouth. Home to Theda Barlow. Lets Her Kids Play Hooky Once Every School Year."

"Freesoil City Limits. Home to Felix Monton, Who Wanted A New Bass Boat But Bought Life Insurance Instead."

"You Are Now In Bristol. Where Barb Dibs Supports The Arts, Even On Her Fixed Income."

And finally, this, on a sign near where you live: Everytown's City Limits: We Still Read The Newspaper."

Rolling Out a Paper Trail

Most of us use it every day, and hardly give it a passing thought.

Unless, of course, it's paltry. Or skimpy. Or scratchy.

Or, worst of all, gone.

I'm talking about a roll of paper that hangs on a wall or stall and can make all the difference in your day.

You know what I mean if you've ever been treated to toilet paper that's nothing more than a series of insulting slips of paper that have to be wrested from their little tin compartment.

Or, conversely, luxuriated in deep, four-ply tissues that almost compel you to share the experience.

Well, allow me.

It was just last week that I was attending a meeting atop the Old Kent Bank building in downtown Grand Rapids. I visited the restroom that's part and parcel of the University Club on the 10th floor.

There, I discovered toilet paper as soft as freshly baked white bread and more absorbent than chamois.

Not that I dwell on such things.

But I'm a man of minutiae, a purveyor of the little things that make the world go 'round.

So I left the University Club that morning with purpose: To discover just what sorts of toilet tissue that establishments downtown stock in their respective bathrooms.

The results, I fear, may bowl you over.

– The Hall of Justice: Much better than what I'd expected from a place that caters to lawyers and felons. A decent two-ply tissue with a raised dot design that adds a certain ambience to an otherwise drab building.

– Grand Rapids Public Library: Nothing special, but nothing to complain about, either. About what you'd expect in bathrooms where, let's face it, patrons can read to their hearts' content.

– Kendall College of Art & Design: The healthy tuition they charge here isn't going into things like toilet paper. We're talking the dreaded seamless roll of tissue that's tough to tear and even tougher on skin. Might as well use canvas.

– The Ledyard Building, in the 100-block of Ottawa Avenue NW: Give this tissue an A. Someone's paying attention to details here; the bathrooms also come equipped with disposable seat covers.

– Courtyard by Marriott on Monroe Avenue NW: Verrrry nice. And when the help gets the chance, they're folding down the tissue's ends into neat little triangles. Almost makes you want to book a room for nothing more than the morning experience.

– Riverfront Plaza Building on Campau Avenue NW: Way too thin for my liking. A close inspection of an unwrapped roll showed that it's "100 percent recycled." Made me think "Hmmmmm..."

– Founder's Building on Fountain Street NW, 2nd floor: I'm standing at the reception desk for the Frey Foundation. Will they let me test their tissue? Certainly, says a cheery Carol Hubbard. In a moment, I know why she's cheery – a multi-layer embossed white tissue that rocks. I could live here.

– Grand Rapids Children's Museum on Sheldon Avenue NE: Tsk, tsk, I say. And John Milewski, the museum's operations manager, concurs. "I'll admit, I had to cut expenses," he acknowledges. Then again, it's mainly for kids, right? What do they care?

– Grand Rapids Community College: A grade above Kendall's, but only because it's perforated.

– Amway Grand Plaza Hotel: It's what you'd expect from a four-star hotel: Fluffy without being pretentious. And yet, at the Amway-influenced Van Andel Arena and DeVos Hall, we're talking El Cheapo. All three ought to get on the same page.

– The Peninsular Club, at 120 Ottawa NW: A swanky joint with classy people both at the helm and as clients. But yow! Why don't they just stock 80-grit sandpaper? Members shouldn't take this sitting down. Upgrade immediately.

– Fulton-Commerce Building, at 38 W. Fulton: Up the back steps I go to visit the bathroom at radio station WGRD. Their paper is downright scary – laced with little amoeba-like implants.

Money Can Buy Fame, and Odd Building Names

DeVos and Van Andel have buildings named after them. Why not the Klodzinskis and Scrams?

On the surface, it might be a good idea to name certain Grand Rapids entities after the family whose donation largely funds it.

A proposal to allow just that already has majority approval of the Grand Rapids City Commission.

But my question is this: Before voting, did commissioners consider doing a quick check of the local White Pages to see just what sort of names might one day be gracing our town's plazas, centers, museums, parks, medical centers and more?

For instance, what if any one of the many Kragt families gave seed money to start up an endowment fund?

It probably would be called the "Kragt Foundation."

What if the Burpees were generous to a gastroenterology concern? Would it be called the "Burpee Clinic?"

And if the Newman and Ison families pooled their resources to develop any one of those charming islands that grace the Grand River, it'd probably go by "Newman Ison Island."

A bridge to it – created by donations from the Ober, Trumble and Waters families – would require that we refer to the span as the "Bridge Ober Trumble Waters."

That's just a sprinkling of what could happen if we let anyone other than DeVos and Van Andel affix their names to stuff around here.

And as you might have guessed, I've got more possibilities, thanks to names – real names – I dredged up from the phone book, then attached to places and things that either do or could exist here...

Moran College.
Hooker Hotel.
Center Center.
Noseworthy Gardens.
Sprung Fountain.
Seymour Eye Center.
Chase Lounge.
Boozer Drug Rehabilitation Center.
Dumas University.

Montee Hall, Monte Hall or Monty Hall.
Poorman's Mall.
Crumley Towers.
Ohlmann Veteran's Facility.
Outen Inn.
Dumbalb Think Tank.
Letts Park.
Butts Smoking Cessation Clinic.
Loose Women's Resource Center.
Soules Cemetery.
Nota Word Literacy Center.
Garden of Eden.
Nocon Dew Arbitration Institute.
Empie Stadium.
Chubb Health Complex.
Hurt Hospital.
Norasing Auto Speedway.
Meaney Humane Society.
Scram Runaway Assistance Center.
Antes Picnicking Grounds.
Louder Broadcast Center.
Loveless Human Services Organization.
Mosqueda Summer Camp for Kids.
Karash International Airport.
Loser Casino.
Tardy Postal Service.
Yow Pain Clinic.
Zito & Zwart Dermatology Institute.
Stump Nature Center.
Klodzinski School of Ballet.
Poisson Regional Poison Center.
Boren Tourist Attractions.
Rott's Farmer's Market.
Polk Blood Center.
Bonk Head Injury Treatment Facility.
Stuck Transit System.
And finally...
...Urena Arena.

True Blue Jeans Lost to 'Haute Couture'

Long ago, before the term "haute couture" was invented to talk people out of wearing Nehru jackets, you went to the store for blue jeans and that's what you walked out wearing.

You walked out very stiffly, of course, because there used to be laws about buying clothes that had been secretly pre-washed by large matronly women who wore hairnets. But you did walk out in jeans. Blue jeans. Jeans that were blue. Simple.

The only mild complication was in assessing your size, including the circumference of your thighs. If you had big thighs as a child, it meant you ate too many Ho-Hos, and the salesperson would sternly usher you into the dreaded "big boy" area. That's where they kept all the jeans that had "HUSKIES" stamped on the right rear pocket.

If sent to the "HUSKIES" section, you would want to dig a hole and hide yourself, but of course that was next to impossible, as Huskies kids required extra big holes, and you'd end up needing help shoveling it out. And everyone would just say no. They'd say, "Dig it yourself, lardbutt."

So you endured the "HUSKIES" label on your backside until it either wore off or you were old enough to afford a leisure suit, whose coats were just long enough to hide your hiney.

Plus they didn't say "HUSKIES" anywhere. They did make a fashion statement, though. They said, "Wearing me is proof your brain is atrophied; shed me or never date again."

Today's jean market, however, has nearly solved these dilemmas. It has done this by offering blue jeans that are no longer blue. They're not jeans, either. They're "denims," which is a French word for "haute couture."

To convince yourself this is no longer The Age of Simplicity, try buying some blue jeans. "I'm looking for blue jeans," I said.

"What kind?" asked a cheerful saleswoman named Renee.

"Blue ones."

She motioned to a wall of shelves, with jeans stacked 8 feet high. I found some bluish jeans, but not blue jeans. Instead, there were baby blue jeans and powder blue jeans and two-tone blue jeans.

"Do you ever get people in here who see so many kinds of jeans they don't know what to do?" I asked Renee.

"All the time," she said.

I studied the labels on the jeans. They said 'Unwashed,' 'Whitewash,' and

'Stonewash' and 'Blizzard Wash' and 'Acid wash' and 'Dry Ice' and simply 'Pre-Washed.' I looked around for matronly women with dishpan hands.

There were jeans with 'tapered leg' and others with 'straight leg.' There were jeans with a 'boot cut' and others labeled 'stretch.' One variety was marked 'relaxed fit.'

"What's that mean?" I asked Renee.

"It's more of a baggy style."

"You mean for big people," I said. "You mean 'Huskies,' don't you?"

There were '501' jeans. "Those have a button fly and straight leg," said Renee. There were '505s.' "Just a basic straight leg with a zipper fly, she continued. And '550s?' "A relaxed fit with tapered leg."

'Five-seventeens?' "Boot cut." And '506s?' "Straight leg, snugger seat," said Renee, "for the real skinny person."

Some of the jeans were blue, but not, well, you know, blue. Most of them were black and gray and white and cream and off-white. A lot of them were speckled, reminding me of bass.

Which is what blue jeans were originally designed for – fishing. Fishing and farming and the laying of carpet. But now, said Renee, "Jeans are worn for just about anything." Most prefer the 'Whitewash' type, she encouraged.

But I wouldn't yield. 'Dry Ice' is what you throw into water to see smoke. 'Acid Wash' is what I kept my hands away from when I ran a barrel plater. The number '501' belongs on a motel room door. And 'Whitewash' is what you put on a fence.

Don't give me jeans that someone beat up with a bucket of bleach. Give me something real, like Ho-Hos. Give me something worth remembering – a big pair of HUSKIES, with rolled-up cuffs.

Give me something I can hold onto; give me a big woman in a hairnet, and room to dance the polka.

CHAPTER 7

Leagues

'It's About Miracles'

To the casual observer, the only thing standing between Matt Hales and a varsity letter was swimming 58 seconds or faster in the 100-yard freestyle.

But those who know him better realized that to launch himself from the starting block one day last week was the culmination of a dream deferred.

Last June and July, the Rockford junior lay comatose with a skull fracture and severe closed-head injury, the result of a one-car accident at Grand River Avenue and Three Mile Road NE.

And now, just nine months later and against all odds, he faced a defining moment: Could he stroke four lengths of the pool in 58 seconds or less?

It's an ambitious goal even for someone who has not been dealt the severe trauma Matt Hales survived.

As a freshman, he had narrowly missed qualifying for his letter. As a sophomore, he had not only accomplished the feat, but been voted Most Improved by his swimming and diving teammates at Rockford High School.

But now, as a junior, well, anyone would have understood had he chosen to not even entertain the idea of trying for such a standard.

All season long, he had been unable to hit the mark. "When I saw him at our first practice after the accident," recalled Rockford Varsity Swim Coach Don Seifert, "I was only hoping that maybe he'd be able to match his freshman times."

By the end of the dual meet season two weeks ago, Matt had brought his time down to 63 seconds – admirable, yet still far short of his goal.

So Coach Seifert did what a lot of other coaches do toward season's end: He set up an official time trial, for Matt as well as other swimmers still trying for a letter.

The first was last Tuesday, and I happened to walk in on it while visiting the pool for another reason.

"Matt Hales is trying for his varsity letter," someone whispered to me, and being somewhat familiar both with swimming and his accident, I was floored that he was even flirting with the 58-second goal.

That day, I watched as he failed by two-tenths of a second. I asked Seifert if that was that, and he said he would schedule one last time trial the following day. I said I would be there.

On Wednesday, I arrived to a veritable fan club cheering for Matt Hales. Some two dozen classmates had rearranged their own schedules to watch his effort. Matt's father, Mark, was there, too, and in communication by cell phone with his wife, Tracy.

Some of his classmates had tears in their eyes, no doubt remembering how he fought his way back from a deathbed following the June 3 accident. He was a passenger in the car, which hit a huge boulder and flipped over.

He had to be pulled from the flaming car, then spent more than a month at Spectrum Hospital, then nearly a month at Mary Free Bed Rehabilitation Center.

Two weeks into his initial stay, they almost lost him. "I feel incredibly helpless," his mother, Tracy, wrote in her journal. "Dad and I are in shock."

His brain was swelling. His carotid arteries were in danger of shutting down. His parents got down on their knees and prayed.

"God has you now," wrote a grieving mother. "It is my hope that you will someday read this journal, but we are in the deep dark chasm of the unknown."

After riding a horrible roller coaster, he finally pulled through. Though he still wasn't able to support his own head on his neck by the time he was transferred to Mary Free Bed, he improved.

And now, he was standing on a starting block, his head shaved in a total commitment to speed, his mind and body fixed on his own destiny.

When he went airborne, people screamed "Go Matt!" and cupped their chins in their hands.

Berk Tanal was another passenger in the car in which Matt was injured, and he was there for the time trial. "I wouldn't have missed this for anything," he said of his friend's resolve. "He's incredible."

Another friend, Dan Paul, observed that "Considering where he was nine months ago, this is amazing."

"This is basically the only sport I can letter in," Matt would explain later. "It's the only thing I'm sort of good at."

"Does this varsity letter matter to me?" Matt's father, Mark, asked rhetorically as Matt plowed through the water.

"No, it doesn't. But this isn't just about getting your letter. It's about commitment, faith and hardship and love and courage. It's about endurance and strength." He took a breath. "It's about miracles."

He was halfway home now, with two lengths to go. His classmates and his father and his coach were on their feet now. "C'mon!" they screamed, "GO!"

He had 25 yards remaining to swim now, and less than 14 seconds to do it. People were chanting his name. And Matt Hales was finally reaching for the wall.

He was reaching in the name of every high school athlete who has ever walked a tightrope between try and try, try again.

He was reaching back, and then as far away as possible from a moment in time that could have destroyed him, but didn't.

He was reaching with a body that mere months earlier could not walk, could not talk, could not breathe on its own.

"I knew there was no way I was going to give up on this letter," Matt said.

"And I knew that if I was to get it, it would belong to everyone who helped me get here. Not just me."

When it was over, he went home. And when he burst through the door, he announced to his mother: "You can take me off the church prayer list now."

Matt Hales went 57.86.

Ball Season, Like Youth, Done Too Soon

The sky was a painter's palette of blues and creams – a perfect watercolor – and yet Matt Heinz, age 8, was burying his freckled face into his father's shirt, softly sobbing.

It had been a great evening for baseball, but with one exception: This was Matt's last game of the season, and his tears were telegraphing to his parents and passersby that it had all happened too soon, too soon.

For those of us who were nourished on baseball – both the ultra-organized type and the purer sort that surfaces on a diminishing number of sandlots – Matt Heinz stands for something grand and glorious and in some sad circles, gone.

Though no one likes to see a kid cry, shedding them over a love of The Game is far too rare and a welcome relief from children whining about their responsibilities or arguing over an allowance.

Matt Heinz stands for our innate ability to understand perfect geometry, to appreciate the musty smell of a rain-spattered infield, the utter abandon conveyed by the space between bases, the outright joy that comes with reaching home plate.

Matt Heinz, even at the age of 8, to be leaning into his father with a tear-streaked face and unable to do little more than nod at others' attempts to console him, stands for all the innocence we once harbored, the way we didn't walk but ran everywhere we went, blurted things out instead of sidestepping issues; perfect youth.

When he packed his head into his father's chest, I think it forced more than one adult on the field that night to pause and reminisce: When is the last time I played hardball? Does it still feel like that to turn a double play? Could I hang in there on a tight curve ball?

And this: When did I suddenly become so adult?

Matt Heinz plays on one of a thousand teams that doesn't matter to the rest of us.

They convene and play and convene and play and these kids – these lovable urchins – eventually blend into other teams. But every once in a while, amidst the ongoing blur, a kid cries for it to be finished too quickly, and

Time.

Stands.

Still.

Because Roger Ferris and I coached the team Matt Heinz is on – was on – we walked over and said things like "It's all right, Matt," and "There'll be other games," but it sounded hollow even as we spoke the words.

In truth, there'll be no games exactly like the ones he played with bespectacled Luke Vincent, whose improvement from game to game was chilling; with Cody VanderWeg, who, even after striking out four times in a row, kept his cool and collected two hits in the last game; with Chris Watrous and Sean Ford and Kalan Snyder and a half-dozen other third-graders who can neither erase the past nor count on the future.

Later on the same night that Matt Heinz, age 8, wept for love of baseball, another father and his sons didn't walk but ran into an overgrown field near their home to play some catch.

An aging Golden retriever served as backstop against the same sky that earlier had unveiled itself, and the sounds we made were those that have been chirped and bellowed ever since Abner Doubleday marked off the first diamond:

"Give me some grounders."

"C'mon, throw the heat."

And of course, there was the three-word anthem uttered by everyone who has ever played the game with true passion, the sort of sentiment young Matt expressed and with any luck, will come to harvest.

While it is the bane of any dad who thinks a game of catch has time limits, the words touch something deep within anyone still capable of remembering when they were 8. And sometimes cried.

"Just one more."

Coach's Move Shows 'Incredible Class'

You read a lot about coaches willing to win at any price.

Not today.

Instead, this is a story about a coach whose attempts to even the score will be remembered perhaps more than any victory his team earned.

And it's a story that should be shared with the high school boys' basketball coach in Oklahoma whose team ran it up against an opponent last Friday, 112-2, reportedly pulling his starters only after the second half convened.

My son Andrew's summer basketball team of 11- and 12-year-olds from the Rockford area was playing against a squad from Freesoil in a tournament sponsored by the American Youth Basketball Tour.

It was immediately clear that the home team from Freesoil wasn't going to win.

"From the beginning," Freesoil coach Steve Rybicki told me Monday, "the outcome was obvious."

Just minutes into the game, Rockford's coach, Vic Villarreal, was already substituting vigorously and plugging players into different positions in an effort to soften the impact. Still, at halftime, his team led 32-0.

After conferring with fellow coaches Mark DeWitt and Kevin Egnatuk, Villarreal approached the beleaguered coach from Freesoil. As they spoke, Rybicki's expression went from dejected to one of disbelief. He looked at Villarreal and said, "You'd do that?"

In a flurry, kids started flinging jerseys. And it became clear that Villarreal had suggested they trade players. Right there on the court. You give me some of yours, I'll give you some of mine. And let's even this game out.

The contest had been conceded. But there was something more important to resolve – how those kids would feel at the end of the game. At the end of the day. Maybe even 10 or 20 years from now.

And not just the players from Freesoil, but the kids from Rockford, too, who relished winning but now had something to prove about sportsmanship.

When I talked to Rybicki Monday, he needed no reminder of that summer day in Mason County.

"It was one of the most incredible displays of class that I've ever seen," he said of Villarreal's proposal.

Rybicki, who also is the superintendent of Freesoil Public Schools and its 135 students, said the lessons that day extended far beyond the 20 kids in mixed uniforms.

"It was a learning experience for everyone involved," he said. "The players, the coaches, and the adults watching."

Trading players is something that Villarreal said "I'd never seen done before," but he knew he had to do something because "I could see in our own kids' eyes that they figured out this game wasn't competitive."

For Villarreal, coaching is a way to help pre-teen athletes do four things: have fun, learn the game, be competitive and try to win.

In roughly that order.

But as the game progressed, "It wasn't fun anymore," he said.

Villarreal, who walked away from the insurance industry to pursue a teaching career, doesn't credit himself with turning the game around, only his players, whom he praised for embracing his plan.

Nobody I talked with could remember the final score that day, just that it was close.

As the gym emptied, "everybody left with a good feeling," Rybicki said. And rather than face a team embarrassed by a final score, he was confronted by something else instead.

Rybicki's point guard, Ross Morang, turned his blue eyes up, and asked his coach this telling question: "When's our next game?"

For One Day, Runners Rule In This Town

Three-hundred and sixty-four days a year, little else stirs the grain fields and Scotch pine plantations here but a rustling wind.

The fertile terrain is punctuated by a thousand combines and gravity boxes, signatures on the landscape that this is farming country, where men and women compete for yield as much with the earth as they do each other.

But one day a year, more than a hundred buses converge near a point that hosts the intersection of four rural counties, and runners spill from the yellow vehicles.

They hail from more than 90 high schools and middle schools to test themselves in the Carson City Cross Country Invitational.

Twenty-six years ago, when cross-country was dismissed as something you did if you couldn't play football, 12 teams showed.

Training techniques have changed since then. So have coaching methods. Diet and nutrition play bigger roles. And Web sites provide teams with everything from pre-meet registration to instantaneous results.

But perhaps the biggest change to confront cross-country is a newfound respect among those who used to sneer.

In some locales, it's even making news, though that's never been the point.

"Runners don't run for headlines," says Don Baese, a long-time teacher and coach at Carson City-Crystal High, whose idea it first was to hold an invitational just outside this town of 1,200.

"Any runner knows that you run for the team, and that you run for yourself, for personal improvement."

And of course, he's not talking about a mere stopwatch. Cross-country tests something more than your ability to outpace a sweep second-hand.

It helps sculpt you as an individual, demanding first that you compete entirely in the open. No companion lineman to help you open a hole. No one to set a pick. Just you to run that last excruciating leg to the finish.

Maybe that's what now draws nearly 3,000 runners each fall to a place like Carson City, a Montcalm County burg where one day a year, runners rule and the whole town knows it.

"Goin' to the track meet?" a fellow pumping gas asks another. "Just turn right at the Amoco station and follow the signs."

They direct you to a surreal scene. On three separate parcels engulfing 289 acres that include two farms and the Fish Creek Sportsman's Club, a sea of buses delivers waves of thinclads.

The local Lions Club parks cars, and there are hundreds of them, carrying proud parents among the growing cadre of fans.

"As this meet grew," remembers Baese, "we ran out of personnel. But people here pitched in. It takes a lot of work, but we're willing to do it, to do anything to showcase the sport.

"Over the years, we've been able to create something special."

Competitors hail from as far away as Cincinnati, and big-town teams with familiar names rub shoulders with lesser-knowns such as Mio, Jonesville and Pittsford.

On a field normally reserved for shooting skeet and trap, they pitch shade tents displaying team names, and it resembles a scene out of Camelot, flaps and flags waving in the country breeze.

Around a former Christmas Tree farm they run, and not for those headlines, or because there was a pep rally in their honor, or on account of how the cheerleaders made them box lunches and promised they'd show.

No throng mentality. No blaring trumpets or halftime show or absurd metaphorical references to "gladiators" or "combatants."

But on an open field like this, picking your way through sandy loam and tall grasses, you discover something about yourself that no court or diamond or gridiron might allow.

One pair of legs at a time, cross-country challenges the true mettle within, tests a person's affinity for intrinsic rewards and little else, promises unbridled opportunity to know one's self.

Who ran fastest at last Saturday's Carson City Invitational? How did your team do? Who captured headlines?

Don't look here.

They run for something else.

'Gimme an A' 'Gimme an R' 'Gimme a T'

If you tour high school athletic fields in your locale this time of year, chances are you'll spot signs that advertise for fall sports.

Don't miss the deadline for physicals, they caution. Football practice begins soon, they trumpet. And inherent in their message is a cautionary note that space is limited. Players will be cut.

As usual, however, classes in music and art and literature hardly whisper their impending arrival on the autumn landscape.

And why should they? After all, our come-one-come-all attitude toward the fine arts has made it ridiculously easy for anyone to come on board.

Choir? Get in line.

Band? Join the throng.

Life drawing? Charcoal's over there; help yourself.

But here's some food for thought: What if the roles for sports and the arts were reversed?

Consider for a moment what sort of mindset students would develop if, suddenly, they had to "try out" for art class. For band.

For Shakespeare?

Conversely, anyone who wanted to play basketball or compete in gymnastics could. There would be no tryouts. And there would be no cuts.

(True, some sports don't abide by cuts, but that's the exception to the rule, especially in larger school systems).

Imagine driving by your high school one fine summer day to read the following on the marquee:

"HAWTHORNE & TWAIN. HELL WEEK BEGINS AUGUST 21."

If you're asking yourself who Hawthorne and Twain are, you probably played too much football. At the very least, you probably missed "The Scarlet Letter" and "Huckleberry Finn."

Just imagine, though, if you'd attended a high school where conversations like this one ensued on a typical Friday morning ...

"Hey Paul, goin' to the pep rally tonight?"

"Duh! As if I'd miss that! After all, you don't just let your school's debate team head to the conference finals without a huge send-off!"

"I hope there's a bonfire!"

"No doubt!"

Or this ...

"Suzie, wanna help us make box lunches for the chess club's big tournament tomorrow?"

"You betcha! As long as you promise to help me decorate the lockers of the guys who made it into Industrial Arts this season."

"Deal!"

Over time, the athletes at school would be taking a back seat to the computer gurus. Belonging to the Varsity Club would be a yawner. But guys who made Latin Club would be looked on as somehow ... more virile. Home Ec would come back into vogue; women would learn how to sew again, and to the praise of the masses.

There'd be tailgate parties at Odyssey of the Mind competitions. Raucous cheering for students who earned awards in silkscreening, photography, batik.

Who knows? Over time, schools might even be able to affect media coverage. Instead of broadcasting football games, radio journalists might show up to do play-by-plays at grammar competitions ...

"This is Barry Appositive, broadcasting the State Finals in Sentence Diagramming. Jimmy Morley of Compound Complex High School is up, and he's got a whopper of a declarative to dissect. A hush falls over the crowd of 8,000. He's got a noun, now a verb ... direct object ... an indirect object ... oh wait – he's pulling off a prepositional phrase. Lookit this kid go!"

Baseball coaches wouldn't be hot interviews as much as the teacher who mentors Glee Club:

"We've got a good crop this year, with eight returning seniors and a JV team that's showing some good stuff in the wings," says Ms. Treble Octave, who is in her ninth year at the helm ...

At class reunions, students would gather in groups to recall glory days played out in the band shell ... on stage ... in oratory.

But none of the above will ever happen if we continue making the arts so freely accessible – and sports teams so elitist.

See ya at the pep rally. And be sure to bring your slide rule.

Glory's On The Water
For Teams Who Row For Speed

The day broke mostly gray and blustery, a veil of fog suffusing morning light. But slicing through the quiet pall that blanketed the Grand River Saturday were thin slivers of men and women gaining, gaining.

There were winners. There were losers. But all walked away with another dose of whatever it is in their guts that makes rowers row. Nothing less than religion.

Some of its devotees describe it as a Herculean test of the human spirit, to condition oneself into the beyond, then put it all on the line in a single 2,000-meter challenge.

Others say it is nothing less than religion, a communion of shell and still water, the oarsman a distant third party as he gently applies blade to water, then switches gears to demand everything from arm and quadricep.

Few are able to define it in a closed, consummate manner. Not in books. Not in tapes. And not yesterday along the banks of Riverside Park, where Grand Valley State University took on MSU in a spring regatta that treated some 300 onlookers to 14 contests, mostly won by Spartan crews.

"I've been racing for 25 years, and I don't know," says Laker Coach Richard Laurence, asked to explain the fascination.

But his attraction to the sport must go deep. Why would he give up a good job with Boeing Co. and the lifestyle that comes with living in Seattle? To put in 1,700 hours in exchange for an annual coaching salary of $12,000? For road trips to New Jersey, Wisconsin, Pennsylvania? For getting up at 5:30 five days a week, nine months a year; to motivate kids doing the same?

For the right to represent a college which that doesn't acknowledge its 65-member crew team as a varsity sport, but instead, a "club?"

He looks across the Grand as if for answer. Another race is under way, having set out from the Ann Street Bridge upstream to a finish line about 11 miles to the north. "I love being on the water," he says finally. "And it's a sport with no stars.

"You win, and you lose together."

Out on the river, 4- and 8-person crews pull in the same methodic way they have been pulling since 1829, when Oxford and Cambridge dueled on the legendary Thames that bisects London.

In the United States, rowing is the oldest intercollegiate sport, with a history dating back to the 1850s. Equipment has evolved from heavy hulls of wood to space-age carbon components costing upwards of $20,000. Training techniques have grown up, too.

But it's still a man or woman's mettle that counts first, last and ultimately. It's the ability to ignite with the command "Ready, Go!," or in more traditional settings, "Etesvous pret? Partez!"

In just the space of 2,000 meters, you must pull as one from the onset, beginning with perhaps three 3/4 -strokes, then shifting into two full strokes followed by 20 power strokes at a rate of 42 per minute.

As muscles explode and the heart responds in accompaniment, the rate might fall to 36 strokes per, then shoot up again in the final 250 meters to a rate of 40.

And this demonic symphony in motion is not over until the coxswain – that voice in the stern who serves as steering wheel and metronome – signals an end to the brutality with "Weigh enough!"

Ryan Quick is a senior at Grand Valley, 23 and majoring in sports medicine. "How can I explain it?" he repeats. He begins several sentences with "The feeling of . . ." and delivers up, possibly without even knowing, a series of paradoxes.

Where Quick and his teammates train, on a sheltered stretch of the Grand just east of the Grand Valley campus, their aquatic track is nearly always calm. "The water," he says, "is like glass." And in the next breath, he talks of mists boiling just off the surface.

Quick and other rowers bundle up against 10-degree days, then shed layers as the body warms. Some winter days, faces and arms glow red, but oars at rest grow skins of ice.

"At practice," he says, "we see the sun rise every day."

It's All About the Ballgame

Let's travel back, shall we, back to a time when boys played baseball for the joy of it, when uniforms sometimes meant a cap at most, and parents not only played a minor role, but actually chose not to live vicariously through the lives of their little ones.

The year is 1937, and Jim Rooney can close his eyes and view his team as though it were yesterday. There's Byrne Phillips, with forearms big as Popeye's. And Billy Tournell, sporting that loud shock of blond hair. Yonder is Dick Howell boasting his favorite striped shirt, and stocky Red Kiehl, and Marv Kuzawa and George Chihock and Hrayer Agabagian and so many more.

They had no formal coach. They had little transportation. And when it came time to finance uniforms, no single business on the West Side could afford it alone, so the kids sought a little something from more than a dozen – Matthew's Drug Store and Rudy's Market and Buttercup Bakery and Fred the Barber and Stan Davis Shoe Repair, to name a few.

"Bob Berles ... came up with the idea to solicit merchants on Bridge Street one by one," recalls Rooney, "with each merchant to purchase one jersey on which his name would be embroidered and a generic cap. I wore Rudy's Market jersey."

Rooney's team played under the auspices of the American Legion, which furnished one umpire, a couple of bats, the catcher's equipment and two new baseballs, one of which would be rewarded the winning team.

Teammate Jim Bush's father, Augie, a former semi-pro baseball player, attended some games, according to Rooney's recollection. But as a rule, parents rarely attended. "Minimal" was how he remembers it.

The kids' fathers did pitch in, though, to transport the kids when Rooney's team won their age bracket, and was rewarded with a trip to see the Detroit Tigers beat the Washington Senators 13-5 at Detroit's Navin Field.

Rudy York caught for the home team. The legendary Charlie Gehringer played second, and Roxy Lawson pitched for the winners.

Rooney is a recently retired manufacturer's representative in the housewares industry.

He communicated with me about his 1937 team for no specific reason, except to note that "We succeeded without an overbearing amount of supervision. We learned how to organize a team, finance the jerseys ... show up on time for games and practices, and how to win through teamwork. But most importantly, we had fun and created long-term friendships and great memories."

Rooney has grandkids in Little League. Like me and a lot of other dads and moms with kids in the same organization, he hopes that the amount of adult involvement doesn't teach kids to become overly dependent.

I'm proud to say that the Little League in which my own boys play has only fostered a growing love for the game. I know this, in part, because my 9-year-old and his brothers and cousins play pick-up games with nobody looking. And I know it based on how he answered me when I went to tuck him in on the same evening I spoke with Rooney, upon asking him what he liked best about baseball.

I wondered whether he would zoom in on the miniature trophies they receive at the end of the year, or the snack parents provide at every contest.

I wondered if he might get technical, and focus on split-finger pitches or pivoting to complete a relay throw or the best way to hide your forward hand on a bunt.

But he gave me an answer that perhaps Jim Rooney might have given his own dad upon being tucked into bed during the 1930s.

In the dark, my son turned to me and answered as though I asked the dumbest, most obvious question in the world.

"The thing I like best about baseball?" he returned.

"Dad, the game."

Whiffleball, Ghosts What It's All About

It's been forever since our sandlot was taken away. A tidy ranch house now stands where we used to play with abandon, inhaling a pure freedom today's kids will never know.

Blame it on organized sports. Housing developments. Recreation departments. Safety nazis. Progress.

But don't doubt it. Just ask any young kid playing baseball what "no bottlecaps" means. What ghost runners are. And "do overs," and playing "500," and how come one kid always kept a roll of electrical tape in his pants pocket when the gang played whiffleball. Come to think of it, what's a whiffleball?

This isn't a slam against the intent of youth sports today, just sadness for some of the fallout.

Well-meaning adults can't be blamed for adulterating baseball and other forms of play. On the contrary, their aim is to provide more and equal opportunity.

Along the way, though, they've helped create an entire generation of kids who expect full-service sports.

Consider, for a moment, how we adults sign up the kid, provide him with a sponsor and/or uniform, schedule his games, conduct his practices, set rules, arrange schedules and worst of all, umpire or ref their contests. And don't forget the "elite" teams we adults have crafted to separate budding superstars from the also-rans.

(Just in case you're interested, a study begun some years ago asking school teachers and coaches to predict which athletes would excel at the high school level. The results of the study recently were aired, after those same kids entered secondary sports. The predictions were only 25 percent accurate. So much for trying to pluck the cream of the crop before they've even reached puberty.)

It all seemed easier on sandlots, where kids reigned and ruled. And it also was where kids learned about conflict resolution, which they now absorb in classroom settings. Hardly room for bats and balls there.

Meanwhile, out on the ball field, instead of calling for a "do over," which makes perfect sense, coaches, parents and umpires argue over everything from a balk to a foul.

Pickup games – the very essence of what it means to be a kid – are dying.

But just in case your child may consider giving it a try, you should know about the talk I had the other day with Billy Davison, who grew up to be William Davison but never lost his sense of play.

The rules are simple

Bill and I were just two of the multitude who played baseball every day, either in the street in front of our homes, or on a sandlot at the northeast corner of Sibley and Glenhaven NW.

Bill and I reminisced for a while about what you'd need to know, should you want to go back in time . . .

1. If you're going to play, you've got to designate home team. No adult required, just a bat. Two guys face each other and one throws the bat in the vertical position at the other. He catches it, then the two alternate climbing it hand over hand. First one to the top wins, and "bottlecaps" means to clamp a hand over the bat's top. Whether to allow bottlecaps must be decided before tossing of the bat.

2. If a kid's whiffleball splits these days, daddy runs off to buy a new one. Uh-uh. Keep a roll of tape on hand and wind it around the break.

3. Ghost runners are necessary when moms have the nerve to call kids in for lunch at different times. Ghosts round the bases same as the batter does.

4. You go everywhere by bicycle, and you learn to slip your glove over the bat and straddle the whole combination across your handlebars. The ball goes inside your T-shirt.

5. With only eight defensive players, right field is an automatic out (reverse for left-handed swatters).

6. No first baseman? Call "Pitcher's hands (or mound) as good as first."

7. Over Mr. Soltysiak's hedge is a homer. In the hedge is a live ball, and a test to see how tough you can be in a thicket.

8. When you can't get a game up, you play pepper or 500 (aka Five Dollars) or Home Run Derby or Move Up Peggy or Over The Line or Three Flies Up. In any case, don't go home before the streetlights come on.

9. Minor injuries do not get treated with ice. They are allowed to swell to the proportions God intended, and worn like badges of honor. Deal with them.

10. Bases? Bases, schmases. All you need is some paper plates or smashed cereal boxes. Or even Scotty Winkel's shirt. His ma don't care.

Runners Make Great Strides –
And Inspire Others

In an era marked by winning at all costs, high school seniors Wallace Gaunichaux and Rob Kleinjans are like breaths of rarefied air.

Neither has ever come even close to knowing what it's like to break the tape at the finish line of a cross-country meet. In fact, both typically place last in their respective conference races.

But they keep coming back for more, and it's like a scene reminiscent of the movie "Rudy" to see them struggle toward the finish line, so long in their arrival that some spectators are already headed for home.

They are not into cross-country for fame and glory. For Wallace, of Kelloggsville High School, and Rob, of Hudsonville High, it's about team, pride and self-respect. It's about personal best.

"My dad," says Wallace, "kept telling me that I just had to keep going, even if I had to walk, and that I'd be better in whatever I do."

As a freshman, Wallace did walk at times. But he never stopped, finishing every race, even though it sometimes took him upwards of 40 minutes – more than twice the time required by the area's premier male runners, who cover a 3.1-mile course in 16 or 17 minutes.

Rob Kleinjans used to serve Hudsonville's runners as team manager, but this season his coach talked him into putting on a uniform, instead of putting them away. Last week, he nearly broke into tears as he recalled that decision.

"My whole team has been great," he said. "They really supported me. Every race, I seemed to improve."

Coaches for both young men agree that Wallace and Rob demonstrate the true meaning of sport at this level.

"We all get caught up in the importance of wins and losses," says Hudsonville Coach Bruce Kunzi, "but Rob represents the essence of high school sports, of sport in its purest form."

Kelloggsville Coach Ray Antel agrees, adding that runners such as Wallace and Rob serve to inspire others in ways that go beyond blue-ribbon performances.

There are tangible benefits as well. Both Wallace and Rob have shed weight since joining their squads. Wallace waves goodbye to about 30 pounds each season, and Rob now wears pants two sizes smaller than he did when the school year started.

But the lasting effects they have on family and fans represent perhaps the greatest gifts of all.

Kathy Hanes, whose son competes for Allendale High School, is among those who always waits for Wallace to finish, no matter how long. "Definitely an inspiration," says Kathy, who acknowledges that because of Wallace, she now walks regularly for exercise.

Rob, too, usually has a band of fans awaiting his arrival. And they always include his brother and teammate Brad, who's younger and faster. It's Rob who got Brad's votes in all three special categories to be honored at teams season-ending banquet, including "Most Valuable" and "Most Improved."

Wallace also has a twin brother who fares better at sports. But their mother, Carla, points out that Wallace "never gets down about it."

Instead, she says, "He just works harder at what he wants to accomplish."

Both athletes earned a letter this year in cross-country. Rob's was awarded for the work he performed three years as manager, combined with meeting the challenge to come out for the team. He nearly changed his mind after his first race – which he took him 48 minutes to complete in 94-degree heat. He walked, but he finished.

Wallace was awarded a letter last year – not for setting any records, but for serving as a role model. For putting one foot in front of the other, no matter how long it took to get there.

Carla says that buying her son's varsity jacket "was the easiest Christmas gift we've ever purchased. He earned it and wears it with pride. And it gives us nothing but joy to see him enjoying his high school years."

Wallace, says Carla – and she could be speaking for Rob as well – "knows he'll never be the first to finish, or even get a medal. But he's determined to never be the first to quit."

CHAPTER 8

Losers

Thief Steals Memories of Mom

BLENDON TOWNSHIP – Melanie Worthington knew she did not have long, so in her last days, she crafted a keepsake for her 5-year-old son that was sure to live on for years: videos of the two of them.

They were not high-tech or fancy. Just soft images of a mother and her only child playing cards, sitting at the picnic table, enjoying a story like "Oh, The Places You'll Go!" before Theo fell asleep in his dying mommy's bed.

"She was so afraid that he wouldn't remember her," said Melanie's mother, Carla. And now, he might not.

That's because someone stole into the Worthington home in Ottawa County and filched virtually every one of the video remembrances.

Detectives have no suspects in custody, and the family has no duplicates of the tapes.

"I can only imagine myself in that situation, and wanting to get back the last images of a loved one," said Detective Lt. Mark Bennett of the Ottawa County Sheriff's Department.

"The (tapes) are probably of no value to anyone else, but of extreme value to the victims."

Bennett wouldn't rule out the possibility that the theft might be connected to recent break-ins in neighboring Allegan County. But he emphasized no arrests have been made.

A single mother, Melanie lived with Theo, an older sister and her parents in a ranch home on a dirt road in Blendon Township. She died Thanksgiving weekend at age 39 of pancreatic cancer, but not before creating memories for her son.

"When Melanie found out she was sick, she wanted to use the camcorder to make tapes for her little boy," her mother said. "So we taped her making cookies with him, playing up at the cabin, anything that he might need to look back on and see how they did things together."

On or about Dec. 10, someone walked through an unlocked door leading to the bedroom that Melanie shared with Theo, according to police. The items taken included two camcorders, a portable DVD player and assorted tapes.

"We tore the house apart," Carla said, wondering if the thief might have tossed the tapes before exiting.

Realizing that the tapes apparently were taken during the theft cuts deep. "It was like someone had come out and taken her away from us a second time," says Melanie's sister, Marnie, 43, breaking into sobs.

Theo still has trouble talking about his mother's death, but follows his grandmother's prompt in professing that he loved his mom "High as the sky and deep as the sea."

Melanie had her own cleaning service, dubbed "Melanie Maids," and counted nearly two dozen customers as her own. "She loved it, and her clients loved her," Carla said.

Both Carla, 61, and her husband, Phillip, 63, are on disability, but scratched up enough to offer a reward of up to $200 for the return of the merchandise and tapes. Anyone with information is urged to call the Ottawa County Sheriff's Department at 800-249-0911.

"Maybe this is one way we can get them back," Carla says of the reward for a little kid's stolen memories. She dabbed at her tears, and glanced Theo's way. "I guess I'm hoping for some kind of miracle."

Thieves Who Stole Letter Add to Anguish of Losing Brother in Vietnam

When Kelly Hage met his death in Vietnam nearly 35 years ago, it robbed him of potential and possibilities. He would never attend college, never fish again with his father or dance with his mother, never return to marry the girl back home.

What he left behind however, was tangible evidence that he had lived and loved, and in a letter, he passed on the simple lessons he had learned to a younger sister, Shawn, just 17 at the time of his death in the summer of 1968.

She treasured what he had put to stationery, especially the parts about how you must cherish the summers of your youth, and hold tightly to friendships. Most important, Kelly told Shawn, was that you be a giver.

She received the letter the day after the family was notified that Kelly, who had starred in three sports at Kelloggsville High School, would be flown home in a flag-draped casket.

Shawn kept the letter in a box that safeguarded it from fire. What she never bargained on were thieves who broke into her home last September.

She would have been able to stomach the fact they took guns and coins and other valuables.

But they took the box as well, even though it only contained personal documents and a big brother's advice.

It's still missing. And Shawn Wise, 50, still weeps to recount its loss.

Her grief was especially magnified earlier this month after reading of the 400-plus break-ins to which a Spring Lake man has confessed. Erik Rivera is jailed and awaits sentencing after pleading guilty in Berrien County to charges of racketeering.

Rivera, who reportedly worked with a band of henchmen who fanned out as far north as Traverse City and south to Kentucky to invade homes, was apprehended before Shawn's loss, so officials are fairly certain he didn't have a direct role in the break-in of her Wayland home.

Still, Rivera or not, the loss of things that can be replaced through insurance rarely is as painful as enduring the loss of sentimental items.

"He gave so much of his life that day, the life he could have had," says Shawn, reflecting on her brother's sacrifice. "Everything he gave, and then to have his letter taken by people who will never understand the meaning of 'give.'

"They just take."

Kelly Hage was the kind of kid you wanted for a son, a brother, a buddy.

Shawn opens a photo album, and there he is, posing in cap and gown with best friends Bobby Pavlovic, Buddy Pierce, Fred Fellows, Mike Nickels.

Before Kelly enlisted, the five of them would play spoons on Saturday evenings at the Hage house. After Kelly died, it was just a foursome, and the spoons never rang the same after a land mine exploded beneath the Jeep in which Kelly was riding.

Shawn still remembers the day a cab came to take her brother off to the airport for his last tour of duty. A voice, she says – possibly the Holy Spirit – told her to run to the window and watch him go.

"Go look," it whispered. "This is the last time you'll see him alive."

The letter arrived that same summer, shortly after the family learned of his death.

The Vietnam War Memorial bears Kelly Hage's name. So do memorials set up by his family. A scholarship is still awarded annually to a deserving Kelloggsville High School student.

But a letter to which a little sister tried holding fast is gone. Perhaps forever.

And the culprits remain at large, roaming the home of the brave.

Cat-Napping Makes Girl Grow Up Fast

This is the story of a darling little girl, a newborn kitty with blue eyes and how adults can be such jerks.

It all began with a trip to a farm that Tallia Halpern, age 5, took last month with the rest of her kindergarten class from Walker Charter Academy. It's become something of a tradition with grade school kids that when the weather turns autumnal, they go on field trips to see apples pressed into cider and watch pumpkins grow.

This is what Tallia and her classmates did, and to top off their trip, they feasted on cider and doughnuts and then toured the farm, which included a barn.

At one point, kittens appeared. A woman had them in her arms, and when Tallia spotted the one with white fur, tiny brown paws and blue eyes, it was love at first sight.

Tallia's mother, Kris, was accompanying her daughter and the class, and remembers Tallia asking immediately if there was some way she could acquire the cat, though she didn't say it like that.

"Mommy," she said, "can I have the kitty ... pleeeeeease?"

Tallia's two older siblings, Abby and Jacob, both have pets they call their own, so it's not as though the Halperns would be breaking new ground here. So Kris asked, and the woman said it was her intention to give the cats away, but not yet, on account of them being too young. In a couple weeks, check back, Kris was told.

They left their phone number with the woman, and on the way home, Tallia was breathless over the possibilities now surfacing in her mind. She even went so far as to name the kitten, choosing "Belle," after her favorite character in the Disney movie "Beauty & The Beast."

Kris remembers that "every day I picked her up from school, she asked, 'Mommy, is today the day I get Belle?'"

And Kris would tell her "Not yet."

Each night before she retired, Tallia said a prayer that Belle would be OK until she could bring her home. Feed her. Give her water. Love her.

After two weeks, Kris called the farm. She was met with a long silence on the other end.

"I'm sorry," said the woman. "The kitten is gone."

Kris was incredulous. "What?!" she exclaimed. "You gave it away?"

No, the woman answered, and then explained that someone came to the farm, saw the kitten and asked if they could have her. They were told no, that it had been promised. But they apparently returned later that same day and walked off with the kitten anyway. In other words, someone had stolen little Tallia's dream kitten.

Some adult.

Some low-life cretin.

Kris got off the phone, and right there was an excited little 5-year-old wanting to know when. Today, Mommy? Now, Mommy?

And a mommy had to do what all mommies dread – break bad news to her kid, explain how our sorry planet sometimes seems to revolve around social misfits who will never understand the pain they create when they take what isn't theirs.

Tallia's eyes welled with tears. "Why, Mommy? Why would someone take my kitty?"

Kris had no answers.

That evening, after Tallia had finally finished crying, she went to bed, and proved to a world of adults that it's still children whom we ought to be imitating.

Because when she said her prayers, she asked God to bless her little Belle. No matter where. No matter why. No matter who.

Belle's Tale

What's the latest word in the saga of who walked off with little Tallia Halpern's kitten?

A resounding "Meow."

More than a dozen parties responded to a column I wrote last week relaying how 5-year-old Tallia was heartbroken when, after waiting two weeks for a kitten she was promised, someone else walked off with her pet.

The incident played out at an area farm that Tallia and her kindergarten class from Walker Charter Academy visited recently. As the group was leaving, a woman appeared with kittens, and Tallia instantly fell in love with a white, blue-eyed newborn.

The woman agreed to give Tallia the kitten, but only after it had a chance to mature for a couple of weeks. Tallia immediately named the cat after her favorite Disney character, Belle, in "The Beauty and the Beast." She prayed for it every night before bed and waited with all the patience a 5-year-old could muster.

But when it came time to arrange for a rendezvous, the woman told Tallia's mother, Kris, that the kitten had been taken by someone who visited the farm several days after Tallia's visit.

Though Tallia was devastated, readers were obviously inspired by her reaction – to continue praying for her Belle, "no matter where ... no matter why ... no matter who."

Calls and e-mails offering a substitute Belle came in from all corners of the region, including the Humane Society of Kent County.

In the end, though, it was Rockford resident Dawn Force whose kitten Tallia came to finally call her own.

"I read that column and just started crying," said Dawn, a customer service associate at the Bank One branch in her hometown.

"How could anyone do that to somebody?" she said of the cat-napper. "It just broke my heart."

So the same day, Dawn called the Halperns at their West Side home to let them know she had a 9-week-old kitten that was white with blue eyes.

"I swear to God that I didn't steal it," she told Kris, explaining that it was the female offspring of a cat she has owned for two years.

The two parties agreed to meet on Plainfield Avenue NE on Friday evening to let Tallia have a look. When Tallia saw the kitten, "She was 6 feet off the ground," Dawn said.

That night, Belle had a new home and slept right beside her new owner.

Dawn looks back on her gift and ponders the possibility that "if only through a child's eyes we could all live," adding that, "you would have thought I'd given her a million dollars."

Of course, Dawn gave Tallia something far more valuable. She restored her faith in human nature.

She showed a little girl that not everyone takes, and that there is as much joy in giving as receiving.

Tallia didn't get the cat she was promised. But you could argue that she ended up with the one she was destined to own, a kitten that Kris says is even better-looking than the first.

But I think the kitten is only part of the pretty picture that accompanies today's column.

Wouldn't you agree?

There Ought to be a Law...

Everyone knows the jails are overcrowded. Still, it seems there ought to be harsher penalties for nonsensical behavior and general stupidity.

Incarceration, then, for the following, at least until they come to their senses:

– Any parents whose household contains more than three TVs.

– People who think "Quick, pull my finger!" isn't funny.

– Anyone who's not ready to order at a fast-food restaurant, even though they've had five minutes to consider the menu.

– Artsy types who bastardize words like "center" and use "centre." Same goes for "pointe."

– Any homeowner who erects those ridiculous-looking black plywood cutouts of a leaning cowboy.

– People who think the declaration "That's so cool" was first coined during the '90s. Hint: You're about 30 years late.

– Anyone who refuses to give at least a little to charity.

– Tailgaters.

– Any guys with cars cooler than mine.

– Anyone who thinks "acrossed" is a word. It's not.

– People who put WELCOME mats out when you're really not.

– Men who refer, seriously, to their wives as "the little woman."

– Schoolteachers who complain about their 10-week summers off.

– Everyone who complains about teachers.

– People who say, "Hot 'nuff for ya?"

– Gardeners who think you really want their extra zucchini.

– Kids who don't lift a finger for their allowance.

– Parents who don't award their kids an allowance.

– Capricorns.

– People who tan all year long.

– Anyone who stands mute during the National Anthem, unless of course, they've got a terrible voice, in which case, thanks.

– Concert-goers who stand and scream for just one more encore song, when, in fact, they're sick of the act.

– Women, who, upon being complimented on their $800 cashmere dress, say things like, "Oh, this old thing?"

– Anyone who plants a politician's sign in their front lawn.

– Moms who refuse to cook.

– Dads who refuse to play catch. Or, come to think of it, cook.

– Men who refuse to loosen their neckties even though the temperature reads 92 degrees.

– Accordion players.

– People who go tsk-tsk when they discover you haven't read "Tuesdays With Morrie" or seen the latest episode of "Friends."

– Card cheats.

– Bosses who rule through intimidation.

– Mimes.

– Swindlers who peddle a used car without divulging major defects.

– Parents who don't THINK when considering names for their kids, i.e. Harold Armpitz.

– Any band that insists on playing "Proud Mary" at weddings. What's the connection?

– People who stand in doorways to chat.

– Uppity columnists.

Confronting a Killer

There were two things I wanted to do as I strode to the table where I would finally meet Linda VanderVeen's killer face to face.

Show him her picture.

And ask him why.

On Monday afternoon, he looked nothing like the 27-year-old man arrested 30 years ago this week for the death of the 11-year-old school crossing guard from Mulick Park School who was strangled and left dead in a snowbank.

In 1979, Albert Lee was slim and seemed taller. He carried himself with an aloofness that bordered on arrogance.

The 58-year-old Lee across from me Monday afternoon at the Michigan Reformatory in Ionia was much heavier, and he appeared resigned to his fate. He wore a two-tone jail uniform of blue and orange, and dark sunglasses to dim the effects of what he said is glaucoma.

In a large, windowed room devoid of any other people, we sat across from each other with no barrier other than a table.

An armed guard stood in an adjacent hallway.

I was here, I told him, because sadly, this spring marks the 30th remembrance of the girl you killed.

"I did not commit that crime," he said. "I did not know that victim. I'm puzzled just like everyone else."

Actually, everyone else isn't puzzled, but when you're surrounded by 1,200 other men who also claim they were imprisoned unjustly, maybe that's how you rationalize spending the rest of your life behind bars.

Everyone else, as Albert Lee put it, seems resigned to the fact that he was the culprit – convicted not once, but twice, for the crime.

As if on cue, Lee started to run through the evidence that was his ruin, claiming authorities planted material in his car, then perjured themselves. I eventually waved him off. I wasn't there to retry his case. I asked him if he planned any more appeals.

"I'm gonna file pretty soon," he said, his confidence seeming to build.

His mood changed drastically, though, to learn that better DNA tests he hopes for can't be done with any blood or hair strands from Linda's immediate family: mother Shirley, older brother David, and father Andy, who was personnel director for the city of Grand Rapids.

"They're all dead," I told him.

"What?!" he answered, obviously agitated. "Oh, man, no, because I was hoping with this new DNA evidence to ..." – he put his left hand to his head – "... I did not do this crime."

Kent Prosecutor William Forsyth insists otherwise.

"In all the years he's been locked up, I've never lost any sleep over the fact he's in prison."

Forsyth can recite chapter and verse the evidence that convicted a man who once dreamed of being a teacher. Forensics proved that a barrette and blond hairs found in Lee's car were likely Linda's. They found hairs belonging to Lee on Linda's clothing.

Of Lee's insistence he was framed, Forsyth scoffed.

"I fully expected he would tell you what he told you," Forsyth said. "I don't believe him anymore today than I did 30 years ago."

Lee was apprehended about six weeks after Linda's death in February, 1979. He had moved to Michigan from Texas as a teen and worked odd jobs in Battle Creek before earning credits at Kalamazoo Valley Community College and Western Michigan University. He followed a girlfriend to Grand Rapids.

Lee was sentenced to life without parole, and shared that my visit Monday marked the first from an outside visitor in perhaps 25 years. He said he suffers not only from glaucoma, but also diabetes, high blood pressure and prostate cancer.

When I asked him about friends and relatives on the outside, he broke into tears. I only heard something about "a niece and nephew ..."

"Most of my family has passed," he finally said. "You're makin' this hard."

He has been assigned a one-man cell at Ionia. He gets outside two to three times a day. He participates in an Islam-affiliated religion and spends much of his free time reading.

During our interview, he pulled off the dark sunglasses, so I pulled a black and white photo of the girl he strangled with her own necklace.

I pushed the photograph across the table.

"That's the victim?" he asked.

"Yes. Does it affect you?"

"Nah, it don't. No." A moment passed and then he said, "I don't see how anybody could do such a thing like that."

I stood up to go, but first I left him my name and work number.

"In case you ever feel like changing your story," I said.

"What do you mean?" Lee said.

"If you were to confess."

"I would risk my life to save a child," Lee said.

He watched as I scribbled in my pad.

"Are you going to put that in there?"

CHAPTER 9

Lessons

Silver Purse Holds Simple Life Lesson

Once upon a time – well, this past Tuesday, actually – a little girl from Grandville named Olivia Helms, who is 6 1/2, went shopping with her mother, Kristen, and gently badgered her mommy just a bit for a new purse.

The mommy said not today, reminding Olivia that she already had a purse, and that it was more important this shopping trip to get some winter boots. They were at a place called Marshalls, on Wilson Avenue SW.

Just then, a woman that neither the mommy nor Olivia recognized pulled up in the aisle, and overheard the conversation about boots versus a purse, and complimented Olivia on, basically, not throwing a fit. She even called Olivia "a sweet girl" for apparently understanding that this was a day not for handbags, but galoshes.

Then the woman asked a question. "She said," recalled Olivia, "'Can you help me pick out a purse for my granddaughter?'"

Olivia said sure, and pointed to a beautiful silver one with a satin lining that, while not pink (Olivia's favorite color), was a stunning purple.

The woman said thank you, and then moved along, allowing the mommy and daughter to continue boot shopping.

Later, as Kristen and Olivia began to check out, a clerk appeared out of nowhere holding a Marshalls bag. Even as the clerk was announcing "Special delivery for a little girl," the mommy could see through the translucent bag that it held a silver purse.

And she burst into tears.

Olivia's grandmother, Linda VandenToorn, was also present on the shopping trip, and she started crying as well. Mommies will do that.

Olivia, of course, was overjoyed. Boots are nice and all that, but to a 6 1/2-year-old girl, not as nice as a place where you can store your barrettes, pens, bracelets, candy coins, fairy dust and Dora the Explorer sunglasses.

The mommy asked the people at Marshalls whether the woman had used a check or credit card to buy the purse. No, cash. And so there would be no way to send her a thank you card.

When Olivia returned to the home she shares with daddy Brent and younger siblings Ava, 1, and Ethan, 4, the mommy and daddy realized what a "teachable moment" this was, and then coached Olivia about random acts of kindness.

They discussed what's called " a servant's heart," and "paying it forward" and pondered what the world would be like "if everyone would just do one nice thing for someone else maybe once a week."

Like baking cookies for someone, the mommy said.

Or sending a card.

Just thinking of others for a change.

The mommy contacted her local newspaper, not to draw attention to her daughter or the boots or a purse, but the 50-something blond-haired woman who got away, and the lessons she imparted.

"You read about so much bad," said the mommy, "and then there's this."

Olivia brings her new silver purse to Zion Christian School in Byron Center every day, where she attends first grade in Melissa DeJong's room. It's in an adjacent hallway that little Olivia stores her purse in a locker.

That silver purse is on her left shoulder when she comes and goes, though. And when Olivia turns in for the night, her purse is right along for the slumber, which is about as happily-ever-after as it gets when you're 6 1/2.

The End. Or depending on your point of view, The Beginning.

Trooper Knows it Pays to Pay, Pray

Some days are more fruitful than others.

That's what Bruce Cojeen is growing to learn while he makes his way as a trooper with the Michigan State Police.

A nine-year veteran who works out of the Rockford post, the 35-year-old Cojeen was handling a Sunday shift just four weeks ago when he found himself responding shortly after 8 a.m. to an accident with injuries on eastbound Int. 96.

But this story began to unravel a few minutes earlier, when he stopped at a gas station for coffee.

A new employee was behind the counter that morning, and he wondered if she'd insist he accept his java on the house. So he stuck his hand in the nearest cooler and pulled out a container of fruit juice. He'd at least pay for that.

"It was one of those Sunny Delights," Cojeen said. "Sickeningly sweet. I don't even drink the stuff. But I thought that later on I could bring it to one of my (three) kids."

At the cash register, his suspicions were confirmed: She tried to wave off the charge. It happens a lot to cops. Folks enjoy treating them. It makes some of them uncomfortable, though, so Cojeen sometimes steers around the issue by accepting the coffee but paying for something else.

On his way out the door, his day took another twist when a woman holding it open for him said, "I want you to know I'm praying for you."

"Why," thought Cojeen, "would anyone say that to a total stranger?" Still, what's the harm? He thanked her on behalf of police officers in general, but she countered with, "No, no, I'm praying for YOU."

Cojeen thanked her again and walked toward his cruiser, some 25 feet away. Before he even reached it, the two-way radio clipped to his left shoulder crackled to life with a report of a two-car crash.

The station, on Plainfield Avenue NE at Int. 96, was just a minute or two from the scene, near Alpine Avenue. He popped the Sunny D into a cupholder and sped there with lights on and siren engaged.

Upon his arrival, he surveyed two cars that had collided. A woman was pinned in one of the vehicles with what later were found to be minor injuries.

What caught Cojeen's attention first, however, was an elderly man he later would come to know as Eugene F. Schull, of Three Rivers.

Schull had mistaken a highway sign directing him to merge as a directive to turn left. He pulled his '92 Chrysler across a lane of traffic and was T-boned by

Thomas A. Nezwek, of North Windham, Maine.

Coincidentally, both cars were carrying passengers to Kent County International Airport. Before the episode was over, Cojeen would assist the injured being transported by ambulance to Saint Mary's Hospital, and others to the airport.

He also would need to sort out the accident – who was to blame, road conditions, names and birthdates and license numbers and hometown addresses.

Days later, he would receive thank-you notes or phone calls from both parties.

In part, it's because of what happened after Cojeen noticed Schull, 71, leaning against his car.

"He was half-sitting, half-crouched against the fender," he remembers.

"It looked like he was injured."

And in a way, he was. Eugene Franklin Schull was having a diabetic reaction. His body was shaking, and he was in danger of going into shock. Without proper medical attention, he could be in serious trouble.

In nine years as a trooper, Cojeen had only encountered one other diabetic who needed attention. It occurred at the person's home, though, and help was immediate.

Now, here, today, there was only one thing that could help defend Schull from this kind of attack, and it wasn't Bruce Cojeen's weapon, or a nightstick, or all the muscle packed into the trooper's 6-foot, 230-pound frame.

It was orange juice.

Couple Proves Their Faith, Love Knows No Handicap

Saturday afternoon, a proud father and mother took their only child's quivering hands and walked her wobbly legs down more than just an aisle.

They escorted her into a world that might have seemed improbable, even impossible, if not for a groom who refused to marry for perfectly sculpted features, a lilting voice, flawless powers of reason.

Saturday afternoon, Bob VerBurg and Kim Vredeveld married for the sort of love most of us spend a lifetime pursuing, the sort of love that transcends beauty, perhaps the only sort of love that ought to be allowed.

Nine years ago, Kim Vredeveld lay on what doctors predicted might be her deathbed, comatose and severely injured as the result of a one-car accident.

The Holland native, then a junior at West Ottawa High School, had rounded a corner in her automobile and crashed into a utility pole. Though she didn't suffer spinal cord damage, a closed head injury contributed to severe problems with speech, balance and coordination.

Today, she is largely dependent on a wheelchair, and only recently has developed the ability to walk with assistance. But on Saturday, she abandoned her wheelchair, and in a white flowing gown adorned with pearls, struggled down an aisle in her parents' arms to promise a lifetime with Bob.

In doing so, she demonstrated to a world hungry for inspiration not only that she'd beaten the odds, but how true love is rooted in an appreciation for who and what we are, not the cosmetic veneer we see in the mirror.

Bob and Kim met five years ago. Skimming through the pages of a monthly West Michigan publication called "Single File" magazine, he came across an ad placed by Kim.

It didn't rhapsodize about long walks on the beach, something she can only do on wheels.

Instead, it blared forth from the page with brutal honesty. "I have," the ad announced, "a disability."

"I thought to myself, 'That takes a lot of guts,'" Bob recalls.

Moxie is something Bob has had to develop as well. From the time he began speaking, he stuttered, and endured taunts and teasing from schoolmates. "I got picked on terrible," he recalls. "In a way, I can identify with disabilities myself." Ten years ago, he conquered stuttering for the most part.

Kim, who's 26 now, answered Bob's response to her ad, but was hesitant at first, if only because he was 14 years older. Their friendship and eventual love towered over that factor, however, and after dating for three years, they were married in a civil ceremony.

That occurred nearly two years ago, and marked the beginning of a roller coaster ride that pitted them against everyone from insurance companies to federal bureaucrats.

Because Bob's own home wasn't equipped to handle Kim's special needs, she couldn't move in. And because Bob earned too much as a truck driver, he couldn't legally share her dwelling place, which was being subsidized by Housing and Urban Development (HUD) funds.

So they embarked on a plan to build a house in Gaines Township that boasts oversize doors and other touches to assist Kim. It was finished weeks ago. "Finally," says Bob, "we're living together."

To cement their relationship in a sacred way, they married Saturday at First Cutlerville Christian Reformed Church, providing the opportunity for Kim and her parents, Gary and Betty, to walk the aisle with their daughter.

If there was anyone among the 200 attending wondering why an able-bodied man would choose to take a woman with handicaps as his wife, the answer is partly rooted in something Bob's father told him when he was 6.

"We used to collect coins together," said Bob, "and one day, he said that he had a sure-fire way of building up a lot of wealth. He told me that you have to invest in people – and in the Bible."

"I admire him so much," she tells a visitor, with a voice that fairly creaks as she labors through audible breaths to speak. "He's loyal. He's committed. And on days I'm feeling bad, he makes me laugh."

When Kim lay on the brink of death nearly a decade ago, all her parents could do was pray. "They told us to be prepared that if she did make it, she could spend the rest of her life in a vegetative state," Betty said. "In any case, we knew we'd have a different Kim than we had before."

But Bob VerBurg would only come to know one version of his wife, and Betty and Gary find comfort in knowing that their daughter was chosen for her intrinsic gifts.

Kim and Bob's storybook romance has affected virtually everyone who's aided in Kim's recovery. "She visualizes her life as being full of possibilities," says Kim's physical therapist, Shirley Kleiman.

"She talks of goals and dreams, as a wife and possibly a mother."

Of Bob, Shirley observes, "He didn't marry her thinking that she would evolve into the traditional wife ... that she would fill all those roles society expects of you. Together, they'll define her role, and his."

Saturday's tender service took but 30 minutes, and Kim spent two minutes of it just getting down the 45-foot-long aisle to Bob, who was waiting in a white tux. At the close of the ceremony, after the exchange of vows and after Bob had wiped tears of his own from his right cheek, he swept his bride up in his arms and carried her down the aisle.

He carried her away from a life that could have been one of regret, of unknowing and lost opportunity. He carried her into a future that included two as one.

Beloved Golden Retriever is Replaced, But Not Forgotten

Just when you think that you can't love again or enough, a little dog scampers into your life, a dog who not only demonstrates that she wants you, but that she needs you, a dog the color of russet potatoes.

I might not share this chapter in my life, but the outpouring of sentiment that Press readers showed last July compels me to bring you up to date on how you last left me, a man saying goodbye to his first pet.

She was a golden retriever we named Bear, and she had been rejected by her first owner, a man who returned her because her eyes were imperfect.

Some dog owners are like that, I've learned. Don't give me sick or limpy or a meld of color, they sniff. Give me the best.

This dog wasn't. It's one reason I decided to acquire her, agreeing to pay for an operation to help her vision.

Still, she was in the hands of an even more imperfect owner now – me – who dared to give her an occasional table scrap and let her gain a few too many pounds.

But Bear was a nightly salve for any one of us who needed unconditional love. No matter what sort of day she might have had, she met us at the doorstep as though it was the first time, wagging and begging caresses.

My only regret in receiving her from the hands of a man who thought her flawed was that I had not sought a dog a decade or two earlier.

Still, for nearly 12 years, Bear allowed us to be her constant companion. Then last summer, almost as quickly as she had surfaced in our lives, she faded out.

Bear suddenly caved in on a leg she had been favoring, and we had to carry her 500 yards up a sand dune in a stretcher fashioned from a rope hammock. A trip to the vet confirmed she had cancer. You could do it now, he said, or in a week or so. But it had to be done.

I called a family meeting of my wife and three boys, but it wasn't to discuss a pending vacation. We all just sat on a bottom bunk bed and wept, taking turns with old Bear in our laps.

We wrapped her in a blanket and one by one, said so long. I rolled off in a rusty pickup that she had ridden in almost as often as I had.

Sobbing as the medicine did its quiet magic, I smeared her furry body with tears as it went from warm to cold, telling her what a good dog, good dog, good dog she had been.

The farewell column that ran last July generated nearly 300 responses. Many readers sent sympathy cards, and long, tear-laden tales about putting down their own pets.

My editors and I were absolutely overwhelmed, and I promised myself that if we ever got another dog, I'd let folks know.

I'm keeping that promise today, letting you know that I drove last month to a rural home in Allegan County to check out a litter of goldens. "I think the one I call Ruby is the cutest," the woman told me over the phone.

When I arrived, nine pups were doing awkward cartwheels in the front lawn. One immediately came running to me, and attached herself to my pant leg.

I looked up at the lady and she smiled. "That's Ruby," she said.

It's Cedar now. She belongs to us and we belong to her. Her paws are like mallet heads, and before long, she will be grown.

For now, though, she's a first-time puppy for three boys, none of whom is yet a teen-ager. When they run with her, it's like watching art explode across a canvas.

If we are all lucky, she will grow alongside them as they make their individual treks through high school, college, maybe even courtships.

What counts more, though, is that they learn a lesson perhaps dogs teach best: It's not about love as much as it is devotion.

It's not about getting so much as it is about giving.

It's not about one inevitable sad goodbye, but a dog's ability to convey so many thousands of hellos. And asking so little in return.

Unsung Heroes Fill Our Schools

Admiration should go to those whose achievements don't show up in the teacher's grade book.

At their worst, high school honors programs pay homage to the institution's quarterbacks, tending to ignore the unsung heroes who blended in so quietly at the same school, that they never stood a chance of receiving accolades at the podium.

You know the drill as well as I. Kudos to the kids in the National Honor Society. The scant few who achieved 4.0 grade-point averages (or better). The ones who earned scholarships to blue-ribbon schools. The students who studied hard (or didn't) and ended up on top, at least as measured by the yardsticks we've invented.

Some schools have attempted to bend the bar in recent years, doling out the goods to those who not only earn superior grades, but also demonstrate qualities like "good citizenship."

"Good citizenship?"

As I look back on my own high school graduation – and consider assorted survivors of others – I wonder if we've devised academic dog-and-pony shows that too often pass over kids who worked just as hard or harder but don't fit into our holy molds.

I attended high school with a kid I'll call "John" who never stayed after school for anything – not to compete in sports or go to meetings or help build the homecoming float. I doubt he ever attended a school dance. I don't remember seeing him at a football game.

It wasn't until years later that I understood he had gone home every afternoon to help on the family farm. It hadn't been his choice, either. It was simply necessary for him to pitch in on a matter of survival.

When it came time for the Springtime honors assembly, he might have been repairing a three-point hitch, or milking cows in the dusky stillness of a cold barn.

Sure, some are able to strike a balance, though it's usually with parents' blessings. But even if he hadn't run on the track team or played in the band, didn't his attendance count for something? Didn't he contribute?

It's with those questions in mind that today, I contemplate another kind of honors assembly. And the awards would go to...

– Troy D., who, whenever he was asked, would gladly jump-start another student's car and never expect anything in return.

– Katy S., who endured a four-year stint with severe acne, and wept every night when kids would taunt her with demeaning names about something over which she had no control.

– Brad V., whose volunteering as a Sunday School teacher went unnoticed by the entire staff and student body.

– Geena W., who would have made a crack cheerleader, but worked a paper route instead, because her dad said so.

– Jim A., who made it to school almost every day, despite suffering chronic abuse by an alcoholic father that would have prompted a weaker person to quit school and board a Greyhound.

– Honorable mention to Gus F., who was teased unmercifully every time he undressed for gym class, yet still showed.

– Virgil C., whose various eccentricities prevented him from gaining status on mainline school organizations, even though he's working on a half-dozen patents for computer applications.

– Sara G., whose ability to perform CPR makes her an invaluable babysitter to the little kid up the street with severe respiratory problems.

– Craig T., who only managed a B average, but whose skills as woodworker rival those of an Old World craftsman.

– Lori E., who has no regrets over taking car keys away from her best friend when she got drunk, even though her "friend" later disowned her.

– Gary U., who never really warmed to history or science, but is such a whiz with small engines that the entire neighborhood relies upon him for fix-it services.

– Heather B., who had the baby against everyone's advice, and managed to finish school. A minor miracle.

– Kurt L., a special education student who was mainstreamed into "regular" classes, and when no one was looking, learned how to tie his own shoes.

Kids like "John," who somehow finish high school while laboring on the family farm, and in the doing of it, get no plaques.

There's Lots to Learn
Outside of Classrooms

In many places, today marks the opener of the new school year.

Or, as it's called in some districts, "First Day of MEAP Training," with bewildered students trudging home and clutching instructions to start stocking up on pretzels, powdered Jell-O, energy bars and sticks of cane sugar to munch on during the upcoming tests, which are HOLY COW – JUST AROUND THE CORNER!

I'm all for testing and validation, but as you might tell, I'm not a big fan of how much weight MEAP scores bear in relating what's really going on in schools, not to mention students' heads.

In July, I had the opportunity to teach a Camping & Canoeing class for students enrolled at Grand Rapids Community College. There were no word problems involving two trains leaving Topeka in opposite directions at different speeds. And I didn't quiz anyone on democratic core values or the difference between a simile and metaphor.

But we did teach one another a little bit about a lot of stuff most of us never had the opportunity to learn in elementary or high school.

I put the onus on every student to share an outdoor skill with the rest of the group. A few immediately raised white flags. "Don't know any," I heard from more than one corner.

Then teach yourself something, I answered, and bring it with you.

They did.

And I was wowed by how much I learned.

Nichole Carroll stunned us with a mini-lesson on Henry David Thoreau, one of our nation's preeminent naturalists. His words, received by light of a campfire, hardly compare to someone in a tweed jacket droning on about him in a stuffy classroom.

Taylor Stonehouse, in asking us to wonder how one might string a clothesline between two trees without tying a knot, promptly did so between a pair of giant oaks.

Craig Hood enlightened us on the benefits – both life-saving and playful – that a GPS unit has to offer.

Allison VanDam and Amanda Stonehouse provided a thumbnail sketch of the Pere Marquette River and its ancient history. We listened to every word. You would, too, if you just finished a five-hour tour of its pastoral waters and banks.

Marissa Towney brought an extra pair of pants with her. Not to wear, but to inflate with air. Use it if you ever get into hot water in deep water, she instructed.

Christine Evans had our rapt attention as she identified the appearance and effects of poison ivy and its insidious cousins. I'll never again walk the same way bare-legged through a forest.

Three of the students teamed up to share with us the finer points of starting a fire. James Friar philosophized on the importance of being a good neighbor to nature's flora and fauna. You know, take only pictures; leave only footprints.

Jackie Gillespie turned Girl Scout and demonstrated several types of knots. Andrew Hauck shared what he knew about animal tracks.

Andy Barker, an infantryman fresh out of Iraq, captivated us with how to tie yourself into a rappelling position with no fancy hardware.

Chelsea "Ariel" Cummiford showed us how to open up to each other through conversation, something not a lot of us do well.

To round out the night, David Jackiewicz provided a hilarious demonstration of how to create the perfect s'more. (Hint: Try it with chocolate graham crackers).

Then, Kari King had us join in on one of those ditzy camp ditties that employ nonsense words. Her little lesson left you feeling as though you were 10 again.

Too bad (insert sigh here) the MEAPs aren't like that.

Enjoy your pretzels, kids.

Grounded in the Family

Our friends Kirk and Linda had just about had it.

Their six kids were going 120 mph in 60 different directions. And we're not just talking school, but after-school activities, sports, clubs, friends, not to mention spats over who got to use the television, the computer, video games, this, that and the other ...

So Kirk and Linda did something that a lot of parents these days no longer have the guts to do.

They grounded them.

They grounded sons Andy and Jeff and Jake. They grounded daughters Lindsay and Chelsea and Shelby.

And then, they decided to ground themselves.

"None of us were connecting," Linda said. "And some of the kids were so busy going every which way, they weren't getting their household chores done until like midnight. I finally said, 'This is ridiculous.'"

The next day, Linda wrote on the bulletin board: "Family meeting, 6:15 p.m."

The kids immediately aired excuses for not showing. Andy wanted to spend some time with his fiancee. Jeff said he had plans. Lindsay argued there was no other time for her to shower than the designated meeting time. Chelsea's favorite TV show was on then.

To Linda, it sounded like this: "Blah, blah, blah."

Be there, she insisted.

At the meeting, Kirk and Linda expressed this concern – that their home was serving more like a repository for wayfarers than it was for a family connected blood and soul.

So, Kirk and Linda announced, "We're all grounded."

The edict took effect last Sunday. It remains in effect through this week. It meant no phone calls. No computer time – especially AOL Instant Messenger – unless required for school. The TV was unplugged. And though friends could come visit them, Linda and Kirk asked the kids to refrain from visiting others' homes.

Let's cultivate the closeness we used to have, the parents implored. Let's be a family once more.

The kids' reaction?

Speechless at first. And then, quiet acquiescence.

Andy, the oldest, realized he would be married soon, and agreed to spend more quality time with his younger brothers and sisters.

Jeff said it was crazy, but necessary, though a bit extreme.

Lindsay thought it dumb – couldn't she at least use the phone? But in effect, she gave her nod.

Chelsea deemed it "Cool."

"What we wanted to point out," says Linda, "is that even when they were here, sometimes they weren't here, especially if they were off watching TV or using the computer."

The kids weren't the only ones who had to suck it in.

Linda's husband, Kirk, has been missing NCAA basketball games and highlights since the TV blackout went into effect.

But the results have been worth it.

A few evenings ago, Linda looked over to see Jake stretched out between Chelsea and Jeff, the two siblings with whom he traditionally spends the least amount of time.

It brought Linda to tears.

The family probably noticed.

What a great thing.

Everyman's Journalist

I don't go out of my way to interview famous people.

Charles Kuralt is one reason why.

The nook-and-cranny newsman, who died in almost apropos fashion on the Fourth of July, hardly ever put his microscope on fat cats and big dogs. He focused on the guy next door, a single floating lily pad, some graying whittler on a backwoods porch.

He would have frowned on another journalist labeling him his hero. But his folksy method of gathering and delivering America's back roads made him at least a faraway mentor of mine.

There was a time when the chance to write about the people of screen and of people who scream enticed, and I covered my fair share. But 10 years ago this summer, when I got the job of filling this space three times a week, I took stock of how I should fill it.

I'd been a faithful follower of Kuralt for some years. And the images that haunted me the most were of the people and places and things that inhabited not pedestals, but cozy corners. Blacksmiths and Canada geese. Indian paintbrush and poets.

Charles Kuralt brought those elements to our TV screens and gave them dignity. He helped us to recognize ourselves in each other, and more the bright spots than blemishes. He made us to listen, too, and one of my favorite flashbacks was his trick of ending his Sunday Morning show with a long moment dedicated to grain waving in the Nebraska wind. He refused to talk over the image. He just let it ride, and I can still hear the wind in those acres of sheaves.

So when it came time for me to deliver 800 words at a time to your porches, I promised myself that it wouldn't often be the Rodmans, the Reagans, sundry idols beckoning from MTV.

One of my first pieces was about an old lady from the West Side who'd had her oversized three-wheeler stolen. I followed with other snippets and snapshots from across the fences that separate our yards, fences that prevent us from knowing who lives down the street.

Let me tell you something. Very few of my columns make the wire services. Some have. But hundreds never go far beyond your La-Z-Boys. And that's mostly OK with me.

I'm often asked, especially by kids, if I've ever interviewed Michael Jordan. I ask them if they've ever interviewed their mothers and fathers. Do they know their parents' birthdates? Do they know how their folks earned their first dollars? Where do their moms' and dads' middle names come from?

In a world impressed by turmoil and titillation on a global level, we have abandoned the begetting and art of sharing stories at their purest levels, beginning with family history. I have friends who do not know their grandparents' names.

Charles Kuralt knew this, and it's why he traveled the byways and two-tracks rather than cramped interstates. To meet Everyman. And when he met them, he asked them to tell him what they did and how come.

It's how he found Mississippi sharecroppers who put nine kids through college. It's how he found the magic of New Mexico, which he once described as "old, stupendously old and dry and brown, and wind-worn by the ages." It's how he found a 90-year-old man who carved wooden carousel horses. And it's how he found a country doctor in Grandfather Mountain, N.C., who told Kuralt about a patient who complained that, "I'm sleeping all right at night, and I'm sleeping pretty well in the morning, but here lately, I've been having trouble getting to sleep in the afternoon."

I'm no Charles Kuralt, but I certainly was lured by what he did; moreover, how he did it. Said former CBS President Howard Stringer, shortly after Kuralt died at 62 of complications from lupus: "He was the first on television to make pieces sing."

After 10 years of columns, that's still one of my own goals, and I have never been convinced to the contrary that the most treasured scores come from some nobody making scarves for kids at Christmas.

A man who squeezes a garden from a jungle of concrete.

Kids who say no.

Dads who play catch.

Dogs that come home.

'The Person Who Did This Wasn't Me'

Hopped up on a case of beer, and who knows how much cocaine, he was living out of his car, hadn't slept all night and was down to pocket change when he walked into a convenience store, presumably to buy a snack.

His life changed, though, the moment he spied a senior citizen with a bulging roll of bills in the pocket – and admitted going for it.

"I didn't know who hit me or what hit me," Jesse Daniel Rae, 27, told me during a jailhouse interview at which he confessed to trying to take $300 from Bill Barnes, 72.

"It all happened so fast," he said. "The next thing I knew, I was in handcuffs."

And the whole world ended up with a ringside seat, thanks to a security camera in the Alpine Township store, which videotaped Barnes beating Rae into submission.

Barnes, who lives in Walker, returned this week from New York, where, after his story first appeared here, he was the toast of town on the "Today" show, MSNBC and "Inside Edition."

Rae, meanwhile, remained in Kent County Jail, where he is tapping friends and relatives to try to scratch up enough to meet a 10 percent $20,000 cash surety bond.

He's charged with assault with intent to commit unarmed robbery, a 15-year-felony. The case is headed to a jury trial, in part because Rae's lawyer, Dennis Carlson, feels the charge should be reduced to attempted larceny from a person, a 10-year felony.

I went to the jail Thursday, not knowing whether Rae would agree to talk. He came to the thick glass that separates inmates from visitors: a slender and clean-shaven young man who looked lost. For a moment, I wondered whether this was the same man in the jail photo taken June 22.

A minute or two into our discussion, his eyes welled with tears. "I'm very remorseful," he said, lip quivering. "It's very embarrassing."

He acknowledged quaffing a case of beer during the day and evening prior and said he took cocaine.

"The person who did this wasn't me. I'd been up all night drinking and taking drugs," he said.

Rae worked for several years in Newaygo County and lists an address there on his driver's license. He was born and raised in Macomb County, on the shores of Lake St. Clair, and recently had been living there with his mother. He said he dropped out of Anchor Bay High School in Fair Haven as a sophomore. His stepfather died when he was a teen.

He worked a spell for his father's excavation company in the Newaygo area and said he had a host of other odd jobs – setting tile, framing homes, roofing.

Now unemployed – "I'd been losing jobs in the Detroit area" – he was living part-time out of his 1996 Grand Prix, where he kept a tent and sleeping bag. In weeks prior, he said he'd been drinking heavily and crashing at the homes of various friends.

On June 21, Barnes said he "drank all night (and) used and abused cocaine" with friends in eastern Michigan, then drove to the Grand Rapids area, where he randomly decided to walk into Next Door Food Store at 4616 Alpine Ave. NW.

With nothing more than pocket change to his name, he walked in "for a Little Debbie, some kind of snack." He saw a roll of bills in Barnes' left front pocket and said he reached in.

"It was spontaneous, an easy way for me to get money," he said. "Something just came over me. I seen the money sticking out of his pocket. My drug-induced state was overwhelming."

Rae said he wasn't trying to single out a senior citizen and said his recollection of Barnes was "nothing but a nice, polite person" who offered to let Rae go ahead of him in line. "If I knew he was of that age," he said of Barnes, "I would never have attempted that.

"I wasn't trying to hurt no one," Rae said. "Even while I was getting battered, I was submissive. I'm not a violent person. Even in grade school, if someone was picking on me, I'd just walk away."

Rae said he suffered a black eye and a bloody and bruised nose, injuries reflected in the jail mug. He said he also vomited after being slammed to the ground and pinned by the store clerk. "I couldn't breathe."

Kent County sheriff's deputies arrested Rae and took him to a local hospital, where he was given a CAT-scan.

Rae's lawyer said he was "stunned" to first meet Rae, because "I thought he'd be a much harder individual."

"It's not what I expected," said Carlson, who's been practicing law for 28 years. "He's meek, quiet and mild."

Rae – whose other known convictions include possession of marijuana in 1991 and driving on a suspended license – said he hopes whatever penalty he serves includes admission into a drug rehab program.

Carlson confirmed what his client told me – that Rae had recently attempted to seek help at a clinic in Macomb County but was put on a one-year waiting list.

"He tried to get care," Carlson said.

Rae said he's viewed the videotape of his crime on jailhouse TV and, sometimes, in the company of other inmates. He said they've asked him "What were you thinking?" His answer: "I was drug-induced."

Rae's instructions from the court are to not have any contact with Barnes, but he said that if he had the chance to address him, "I would like to say that I'm deeply sorry for all the trouble I caused him. He came off to me like a nice, polite gentleman ... and I'm proud of him for what he did to me."

Rae said he's eager for therapy.

"I want to help myself," said Rae, "and be a better person."

Father-Son Duo Finish Cycling Marathon

Little did I know.

For the past 12 years, I've been telling and re-telling the story of Mel and Loren VanFarowe to anyone interested in what it means to write about real people.

As much as anything else, what I do focuses on and revolves around "the guy next door" and how you don't have to look to Hollywood or gridirons or the D.C. Beltway to find the stories that define us.

Back in 1995, I penned a story about how Mel and his adult son, Loren, had just completed an odyssey that involved pedaling their tandem bicycle down every street in Kent County.

Nibbling away at their quest one Saturday morning at a time, they clicked off more than 6,000 miles.

It took them 17 years.

Incredible, yes. And even more so when you consider that Loren has not seen one inch of his travels. Not the brightly hued leaves falling from sun-dappled trees. Or the fresh dew on the fields extending beyond brand-new subdivisions.

He has been blind since birth.

Since that story ran a dozen years ago, I've used that yellowed column to demonstrate that the best stories are sometimes right around the corner and originate with everyday folks in our midst. Postal workers. Salespeople. Moms.

What I didn't realize all that time is that the VanFarowes were fully immersed in Part II of their journey, attempting to travel down every street in adjacent Ottawa County.

Just days ago they finished, adding another 6,000 miles and 12 years to their Saturday morning totals, and rarely at more than 8 miles per hour.

In the humble manner that defines Mel and Loren, neither contacted me about their second accomplishment. The news emanated, then and now, from someone else, which can make a story stronger, purer.

"We've just always been thankful that we've been able to do this together," says Mel, who is 80 now but was 51 – his son's age today – when the two began sharing time together on the open road.

"We were always glad to get out all those mornings, and glad to come home, and thanked God for every day."

"Yes," Loren says from his modest Kentwood apartment, where the two are sitting to recount their marathon tour. "Thankful."

Unlike a lot of bicyclists who travel in style, the VanFarowes wore everyday clothes and pedaled their way on a used, one-speed Schwinn Twinn that cost Mel $85.

While they were careful to wear helmets, they never packed so much as a bottle of water, sandwich or even a tire repair kit. If they had a flat – and they did – "we just walked to the van," says Mel, a retired educator.

As for sustenance, they sometimes detoured into a fast-food joint for coffee or a roll. And they admit to scoring an apple on rare occasions from a roadside orchard.

They survived one serious fall, an end-over-end affair that required medical attention for both. Less serious spills left them dazed but unhurt.

Loren, who works part time in metal finishing, can differentiate day from night but sees nothing. Never has. That's where a father's role takes over, to whisper from the front seat that there's a deer up ahead, and Loren, can you recognize the cawing of the crows?

When Mel first proposed the idea of Saturday bike rides, Loren didn't hesitate: "I was all for it," he recalls.

He was living at home then, and with both parents. Mel, however, was widowed seven years ago from his beloved Emaline. Loren moved out several years ago, after a mutual decision that he needed to establish independence.

That makes the time that Mel and Loren spend together even more special. "It's always been important to him, and that's what made it important to me," Mel says of his son.

Loren nods. "I know my father a lot."

Most Saturdays, Mel would rise around 6, load the tandem into his van and drive from his home in northeast Grand Rapids to Loren's apartment on 32nd Street SE. Then they'd drive to a point in Ottawa County that allowed them to complete streets with a minimum of repetition.

They didn't venture out as much in winter.

They set no records for mileage or speed. And you may never see their feat featured in cinema.

Just a father and son aboard an old bike, one fully sighted, the other confined to darkness. Paving the way together.

Band, Director Shine
as Symbols of Devotion

The small band, and its loyal and courageous director, are examples of what's right with city schools.

Cancer has claimed Ben DeVoe's left foot and part of the same leg.

He can no longer mow the lawn. He has a tough time with stairs. And he doesn't run anywhere anymore.

But he will not be denied his many children, and the opportunity to help them develop subtle gifts into soaring talent.

Ben DeVoe is a band director.

Ten months a year, he places himself before students at Grand Rapids Westwood Middle and Union High schools, doing whatever he can to coax music from lungs and hands that are sometimes more controlled by emerging hormones than harmony.

But a bigger challenge surfaced last summer, when he noticed a lump atop his foot.

"It never hurt," he remembers. "But my wife, Debbie, is a physical therapist, and she told me to check it out."

The first doctor he consulted said it didn't appear to be too serious. But by Christmas, it had grown, and DeVoe scheduled surgery in February to have it removed.

That's when doctors discovered it was cancerous, and recommended a second operation – to amputate the foot and part of his leg.

DeVoe, who has been teaching 30 years – mostly at Union High and Westwood – walked in the day before he was due for the March 10 procedure, and delivered the news to his students.

"There was a lot of crying," he recalls. "A lot of emotion.

"I asked for their prayers, if they were religious," says DeVoe, no easy thing to request in public schools these days.

"But you can't believe how many have stepped forward to say that they would pray for me," he says. "For kids this age to say that out loud, well, that's really something."

He weathered the surgery, though even now, three months later, he's plagued by pain. He waves it off rather than discuss his agony.

He returned to work on April 10, a month after the operation. Upon entering Union High that day, where he directs orchestra, he slipped.

DeVoe's crutches went out from under him, and he hit the floor hard, with his stump taking the brunt of the fall. It split open, and still has not healed well enough for him to be fitted with a prosthesis.

He remained undaunted, though, and for at least one reason:

His eighth-graders.

Before DeVoe went in to have his leg amputated below the calf, his eighth-grade band at Westwood came away from the District Festival with a score of straight "ones," which are the best scores a band can attain. With just 27 members, they were by far the smallest band to attain that mark; other bands numbered anywhere from 50 to 120.

Given his medical condition, DeVoe asked the eighth grade whether they now wanted to make a bid for the state festival.

The competition was slated for May 6, just three weeks after DeVoe's return to school.

That may sound like a lot of time for some endeavors, but getting a band ready for state competition is something that takes months of practice.

Could first trumpets Jake and Ricky control their over-blowing?

Would Chris be crisp on the trombone?

What of Christine on the alto sax; could she control her tempo?

They all said, "Let's go for it."

And so a middle-aged band director propped his bandaged stump on a studio chair and said, "Let's begin."

They drilled those three short weeks, then made the trip to Mattawan High School, with fellow students and teachers cheering their effort.

"That man is a pusher, a driver," Anita Hall, who teaches physical education in a gym across from the music room, remembers thinking.

"His objective is perfection, day in and day out. He gets the most out of his students. Whatever's in it for them, he'll fight for it."

In 30 years, Ben DeVoe has only had two eighth grade teams even qualify for the state festival. So just going was an honor, and he told the kids so.

But they responded with more. For the teacher who lost a foot and refused to take an early summer vacation, they scored one "two" and the rest "ones."

"In 30 years," says DeVoe, "this eighth-grade band scored higher than any other middle school."

You can say what you want about public education in Grand Rapids. Pass notes if you will about white flight and poor leadership and fluctuating MEAP scores.

But know this: The teachers are still teaching.

The kids are still learning.

And some of it can't be measured by raw data and standardized tests.

Only the heart knows.

She Gave Him Hope; He Gave Her Away

GRAND RAPIDS – Following his doctors' protocol, Andy DeVries took a black Sharpie and drew a line across his left thigh. Then, he signed and dated it.

And said goodbye to it.

He had been injured in a motorcycle accident, so seriously that, on that September day in 2002, his family was called together to bid him farewell – wife Kay and their three children included, Jaime, Julie and Drew.

In the week after the crash, Andy somehow dodged death. But he was facing life without a leg.

And just when he couldn't feel any worse, in walked a smiling face asking "Andy, what kind of golf ball do you play?"

It was his physician assistant, Sarah Scholl, and DeVries remembers thinking, "That had to have been the dumbest question you've ever heard."

Still, he answered it, telling Scholl, "I like to play a Titleist Pro V1 when I can find one," given that it's a relatively expensive ball.

When he awoke the next day in his bed at Spectrum Health Butterworth Hospital, there in the midst of a room full of flowers was a 12-pack of yellow V1s.

And, in that moment, Andy DeVries realized that Sarah Scholl hadn't merely brought him golf balls.

She had ushered in hope.

If this story sounds familiar, you heard DeVries relate it to you in person sometime in the past seven years, or you heard it Friday morning on National Public Radio.

As part of its ongoing project entitled "StoryCorps," which so far has chronicled the sagas of about 50,000 Americans, NPR broadcast Andy DeVries' tale Friday. At the urging of a friend, DeVries spent about 40 minutes taping with NPR staff parked in an Airstream outside the Grand Rapids Public Museum.

The bus has been recording stories here since Sept. 24, and ends its stay in Grand Rapids this afternoon.

For more information, visit or call 1-800-850-4406.

DeVries works in development for Calvin College, though I knew him long before he secured that job, when we played on the same recreational soccer team more than 20 years ago.

I'd lost touch with him but had always known him as an active guy who, among other things, played volleyball with as much zeal as nearly any collegiate athlete. I also wrote a column some years back in which his son Drew figured positively and prominently.

As it turns out, surgeons discovered enough blood flowing to DeVries' toes that they decided not to amputate his leg back in 2002. That I knew. But the lessons imparted by his physician assistant were something I was unaware of until NPR broadcast his story.

We spoke Friday morning just after the segment aired, and I asked Andy, who is now 62, to fill me in.

He explained that he developed a close relationship with Scholl while he recovered at Spectrum. In fact, when he was transported from there to another facility for rehabilitation, Scholl wrested Andy's wheelchair from a colleague so she could pilot him to the waiting ambulance.

But, before parting, she asked him to do her a favor.

Her father had died before she had the opportunity to get married – and would Andy walk her down the aisle?

He reminded her that she didn't even have a boyfriend, something he learned during their conversations.

"Someday I will," she told him.

Then, they parted, with Andy considering that, in her special and subtle way, Sarah had once again injected hope into his life. That he would walk again. For himself and for others.

She showed him that he might golf again. And, now, she was adding another layer of sunshine.

Her role in his life so affected him, that Andy has worked since then in conjunction with local doctors and others in an effort to sensitize them to what med schools might not cover.

"You're taught how to slice and dice and take out the bad and make way for the good, but what I learned from Sarah is to give hope," Andy said.

Last spring – nearly seven years after first meeting her – Andy received an e-mail from Sarah, 39, who makes her home in West Linn, Ore., about 20 miles south of Portland.

She wrote that she was engaged to Dan Silvernail, 42, and were to be married on June 20. Would he come?

She graduated in 1987 from West Ottawa High School and lost her father the year before. Her mother, Joan Scholl, along with many relatives, still lives in the GR area.

Sarah now works at Oregon Health & Science University, primarily with cardiac patients "who are at their sickest and in their most desperate hour."

Her philosophy of delivering medical care? "I always try to think 'How would I want my family to be treated?'"

Andy had alerted her earlier to the fact that their story would air on Friday, and she logged onto NPR Thursday evening to read his story online. When she heard Andy's voice delivering the tale before dawn Friday while on her way to work, "I was really overwhelmed," and brought to tears.

Her reaction to the story? "I've now realized that little things – like golf balls – can have a big impact on people."

Sarah met Andy at the airport, and she was sobbing as he strolled up to hug her. It was the first time she had ever seen him walk.

A Very Special Daughter-in-Law

Harold Enoch Lape lived in St. Joseph, Mich., in a little house on Lakeview Avenue with too many curtains and nothing more glamorous than 40-watt bulbs lighting the way.

Harold lived most his life in the home with his wife, Florence. Sometimes he called her "Flossie." Other times, "Ma."

Six years ago, when Flossie died at 73, Harold refused to change a thing. He continued to clean the house on Wednesdays, because Flossie cleaned on Wednesdays. He watered the house plants on Friday, same as Flossie had. He put out the good china and crystal when company came. Ma would have approved.

More than anything else in the world, Harold wanted his home to reflect his wife's special touch, even after she was gone. He used to worry that if he got sick and had to go to the hospital, some stranger would be called in to care for the home. Some stranger who might not clean on Wednesdays. Who might not water on Fridays. That bothered Harold, and he told that to one of his sons, Ron, and to Ron's wife, Ann.

In September of this year, Harold was diagnosed with cancer, and it quickly consumed him. Harold came to understand he was a "terminal" patient, and he went to the hospital in Ann Arbor

The care there was superb, but Ron and Ann could tell Harold was miserable, not only from the cancer, but from homesickness. So Ann decided to do something a lot of other daughters-in-law might never consider.

Ann would move from her Grand Rapids area home into the little house with too many curtains on Lakeview Avenue in St. Joe. She would live with Harold. She would help him clean on Wednesdays and water on Fridays. She would stay with him until the end. It would be two months.

Ann LaReau is remembering that decision. "My husband and I both just adored this man," she was saying. "And the pleasure he got from being able to stay at home, well, there isn't a dollar figure that could be placed on that."

There is, however, a dollar figure on what Ann gave up to be with Harold – $34,000. That was the salary she earned at a job she quit with the Grand Rapids Area Chamber of Commerce. She wore a half-dozen hats there, doing everything from conducting leadership seminars to publishing newsletters.

Ron, 50, is a vice president at a bank here, so he and Ann, 44, would not exactly starve without her job. But it was her job nonetheless, a job she'd held for 10 years, a job she'd cherished and loved.

In staying day and night with Harold, however, she discovered a new capacity for loving. The kind of love that transcends changing an old man's diapers when incontinence sets in. The kind of love which overlooks a tired mind repeating itself in conversation. A love which understands when a dying man talks aloud in the living room, to a partner gone six years.

Toward the end, Ann received coaching from a Hospice program, which helped Harold not only to die at home, but with dignity. Ann was told what to expect from Harold. Rattled breathing. Hallucinations. Finality.

Harold would be the first body Ann had ever looked at. She had only first attended a funeral with Flossie's death; even then, she did not view the casket. "I had never seen a dead person in my life."

The morning of Nov. 26, Ann awoke and could not hear Harold snoring as usual. The rattling, obvious the day before, had stopped. No one was calling for Ma. "I knew," Ann says. "There was absolute silence."

Ann walked in and put her hand on Harold's face. Then she sat down to spend a quiet moment with her father-in-law. "I felt a combination of sadness and happiness all at the same time. Sadness because he was gone, but happiness because his battle was over." Harold was 80.

"I was thinking that if there is a life in the hereafter, that he was brought together with Flossie," says Ann. "That's what he wanted more than anything."

Flossie cleaned house on Wednesdays. She watered plants Fridays. And most Saturdays, Flossie would do away with chores and manage to talk Harold into going with her for a long drive. Somewhere where it was pretty. Somewhere where the sun shone.

Harold died on a Saturday.

I Should Have Been His Friend

The 55-year-old man who died last week in an accident involving a city dump truck lived no more than six houses from me when we were little kids, and I was not his friend.

Now, I wish I had been.

Gregory Siemion was the kid on our street who didn't attend St. James Catholic Elementary School. Instead, he went to St. Mary's, a half-mile to the east.

I'd like to think that's the only reason we never hung out as youngsters. But in my heart, I know part of it is tied to how we made fun of Greg because he looked a little different. His ears stuck out even wider than my own. He wasn't quite as verbal, athletic, part of our in-crowd.

He was 12 when his family moved off Ball Park Boulevard NW in 1966. In all the time he lived there, I can't remember engaging him in play more than a few times.

Which is sad from where I'm sitting, because before, during and after his funeral Mass on Wednesday, he was remembered as the kind of loyal friend we all should have been so lucky to have.

He died May 20 when he collided with a dump truck while on his bicycle. The city driver has not yet been identified, and the accident remains under investigation.

Linda Otherlyn rushed from her job at Smeelink Optical, 941 Bridge St. NW, to comfort Greg as he lay near the corner of Bridge and Fremont Avenue. "Lie still," she told him. You need to think of Jesus now."

She could tell his injuries were serious. His left arm and left side of his head were mangled, and blood was seeping from beneath him. She watched him close his eyes and take two ragged breaths, then go.

"I only knew him for 100 seconds," she said. "And I really do believe that it's changed my life. I'll never forget him."

Neither will dozens more who attended Mass at St. Anthony of Padua on Wednesday morning, friends and relatives who celebrated a "simple" man with a contagious smile and far-reaching attitude.

His cousin, Bob Czerew, said that in going through the belongings of a man who never married, they found old pictures "of a smiling, happy boy." Then he fought back tears to recall that just recently, Greg had donated his entire collection of stuffed animals to a young relative. "He always had such a big heart for children."

Greg graduated in 1973 from Kenowa Hills High School, where he hung out with friends such as Bill Ritzenhein, Mike Cardosa, Steve Blohm.

"We protected him," said Cardosa. "I know that behind closed doors, he struggled," and he noted that he and others were "humbled to see how Greg kept his composure" in the face of adversity. Those obstacles included the occasional bully, never having a serious girlfriend and stepping up to care for his ailing parents.

For five or six years, he lived with them on the West Side. His father, Ray, died in 1999, and mother Elaine in 2006. An older sister, Diana Blouw, survives.

Though he lost his license to drive, it never affected Greg's drive to do for himself. He rode his bike to the bank, laundry, store – and uphill four miles one way to attend Mass at St. Anthony's every Saturday evening.

He never soared in the traditional sense when it came to a career, but he was a good worker, taking on posts at the old Pantlind Hotel, Clark Equipment Co., Michigan Bulb, Kmart, a plating firm.

He rarely traveled. "Going to Muskegon was a big trip for him," recalled Blohm.

"I asked him one day if he'd ever been to Florida," said Cardosa, "and when he said no, I said, 'Well, get in the car,'" and off they went.

Mary Ellen Duffy was a classmate of his at St. Mary's, and while Greg didn't stand out, he was part of her beloved class, and so he was special.

People were mean to him sometimes, she acknowledged, "but he just rolled with it. He accepted people." She remembered him as quiet, "but he was always smiling."

At Wednesday's funeral, which was attended by Grand Rapids Mayor George Heartwell, Deacon Leo Ferguson called Greg's smile "kind of catchy," reminding everyone there how "we all want to have our chance to say our goodbyes, but don't always get the chance."

Or create the opportunity.

I had 43 years to get reacquainted with the kid from the old neighborhood but never took the first step.

I'm glad I had the chance to listen to others lift him up, to describe his smile, share how he treated others, and against all odds. Truly, the meek do inherit the earth.

It was Cardosa who perhaps brought to light a human condition that affects us all – how we lose touch with people who live just down the street, around the corner, across town.

He and the others who were Greg's high school classmates hadn't seen each other in many years, either. "You get married, you lose contact," he said, his sad eyes showing tears.

"And now," he said, glancing at a closed casket just before the funeral began, "here were are again."

CHAPTER 10

Love

Dad's Secret Became Wedding Gift

For three hours, Jim Madsen milled about his daughter's wedding reception, assuring everyone that his mother, Nita Madsen, was fine. Her heart was weak and she had been taken to the hospital, he told those who asked, but only for observation. She was OK.

In truth, Jim Madsen was harboring a secret that he pledged to himself he would not share until his daughter and her groom played out their special day.

And it was this: That his beloved mother, on the way to the reception, died suddenly in his sister's arms. Plagued with a bad aorta for 10 years, Nita had somehow willed herself to witness her granddaughter's wedding, then expired along a beautiful stretch of Knapp Street NE overlooking the Grand River, two miles shy of Egypt Valley Country Club. She was 82.

Jim Madsen insists this story is not about him, but instead a mother's love, and the final earthly gift she was given by God that day to share with others.

But it also is a story of selflessness, reflecting a father's devotion to his daughter and incredible selflessness in the decision to delay his own grief so a young couple could celebrate their union.

The Oct. 15 wedding joined Katie Madsen, 24, and Curt Hoffman, 29, inside the chapel at Reformed Bible College on the East Beltline. Afterward, Nita climbed into the back seat of a vehicle bound for the reception, accompanied by daughter Linda Brouwer, her husband, Mike, and three grandkids.

Halfway there, while laughing and joking with her grandchildren, Nita announced she was having chest pains. Mike stopped the car so the children could exit. Linda – a nurse who had been tending to her mother's medical needs since she was diagnosed years ago with an aneurysm – jumped in back to comfort her.

In less than a minute, Nita closed her eyes and took a last breath against Linda's cheek.

Jim just arrived at the country club when a relative advised him to go back. He did, and decided almost immediately that only those there with grandma should know the whole truth. And that they should soft-sell it to those at the reception.

"We made a plan," Jim says. "And that plan was to go to the reception and keep this to ourselves. We pretty much made a pact that this is what needed to be done. That this is what grandma would have wanted."

Bill Search, a minister who officiated at the wedding, was in on the decision. He had pulled up directly behind the car in which Nita was riding, and witnessed everything. "What a tremendous story of God's grace," he says. "Here's a father who held it together so his daughter could focus on her day."

That evening, Jim figures 30 or more guests approached him personally, and asked how his mother was doing. He and the others answered everyone the same way: "Grandma has a heart situation. Linda and Mike are with her while she's being observed. Everything's OK."

Jim says credit is due the grandkids who also kept the secret until the following day, especially the youngest, Alissa Brouwer, 12, who was at the scene when grandma died.

The bride that night never suspected a thing. Katie Hoffman says she looks back on pictures of herself dancing with her dad, and his eyes are all for her. Through tears, she said, "It makes my heart break to know what he must have been going through."

The song they swirled to? "It's a Wonderful World."

Only toward night's end did Jim allow himself to grieve. He walked out onto the country club's driving range and wept for the woman who raised three kids, who was everyone's friend, who never had much money but always brought beef and noodles to family parties.

Even as he cried, Jim Madsen, 54, remembers hoping no one could see. He was glad he had worn a black tux. He blended right in.

Wife's Role Was Different 50 Years Ago

Editor's note: The Press would like to emphasize that the opinions expressed by our columnists – especially this columnist, and especially this day – do not necessarily reflect that of the newspaper. Thanks for being a faithful subscriber!

It used to be that when the man of the house arrived home, bells went off.

The kids swarmed to greet him. His wife sashayed to the front door. The dog bounded forward in ecstasy. When those wingtips hit the front porch, the world stopped.

This may still be happening in some corners of the world. Saudi Arabia, for instance. Greenland, perhaps – assuming any women and children even live there.

But not mine.

I'm not complaining. Only making an observation, and it is this: There are not enough Mrs. Grinczels to go around anymore.

You may know or know of Steve Grinczel. He covers the Michigan State University sports programs for The Press and the seven sister papers that are part of the Booth Newspapers group.

I went to high school with Steve, played soccer with him for more than 25 years, and we're still friends. And few things compare to the times I would visit his family's home on the lower West Side, and be treated to Old World hospitality.

His mother would greet me warmly, then retreat to the kitchen to make us a meal. The time of day never mattered; she would just automatically produce terrific fare.

My mother behaved similarly. So did Mrs. Davison. And Mrs. Siegel. And Mrs. Scalabrino. The Gryzans. The Kirchhoffs. The O'Briens. The Bechtolds. I could go on.

Instead, I want to share part of a little liturgy entitled "The Good Wife's Guide" that was first published in the May 13, 1955, issue of Housekeeping Monthly. It's been around the block via the Internet ever since. But it really did appear in print:

– "Have dinner ready. Plan ahead, even the night before, to have a delicious meal ready, on time for his return.

– "Be a little gay and a little more interesting for him. His boring day may need a lift and one of your duties is to provide it.

– "Prepare the children. Take a few minutes to wash the children's hands and faces ... They are little treasures and he would like to see them playing the part. Minimize all noise ... Try to encourage the children to be quiet.

– "Listen to him. You may have a dozen important things to tell him, but the moment of his arrival is not the time. Let him talk first – remember, his topics of conversation are more important than yours.

– "Don't complain if he's late home for dinner or even if he stays out all night. Count this as minor compared to what he might have gone through that day.

– "Don't ask questions about his actions or question his judgment or integrity … You have no right to question him.

– "A good wife always knows her place."

There are men – as well as women – who believe that we would all be better off if the above were the norm.

I don't believe either gender ought to present themselves as a doormat when the other arrives home. Taking care of kids should be a shared responsibility. And to dote on a spouse from time to time should be viewed as a privilege, not duty.

That includes an occasional sandwich, even when he or she isn't expecting the favor.

It's just one of those little things that people who love do for one another.

Could I please have mine with extra tomato?

Dog's Love for Master is Unflagging

Before Mike Petchauer died of cancer last month, he asked a friend, Clif Phinney, if he would be willing to care for Petchauer's beloved dog, "Dozer," after he passed.

"I mean, he's asking me this on his deathbed," said Phinney, and he told Petchauer that sure, Dozer would be welcome company for his own dog, Jade.

Two days later, Petchauer entered the hospital with the knowledge that he wouldn't be coming home again – home to the white clapboard two-story he rented at 41 Travis St. NE.

Petchauer spent many an evening sitting on his little porch with Dozer curled at his feet, whiling away the hours in this neighborhood that offered a view through the black wrought-iron railing of not much more than nearby factories and the passing of cars and kids.

On rare occasions, Petchauer and Dozer would be able to see the faintest glow of a sunset in the southwest sky.

Dozer, a 5-year-old Husky-Malamute mix, was rarely far off, since Petchauer worked at a business attached to his dwelling, a convenience store called Tillie's Market, around the corner at 1702 Monroe Ave. NE.

Every now and then, though – sometimes when Petchauer was just inching open the front door – Dozer would bolt.

"That dog loved to run," said Mike Siwek, the owner of Tillie's who hired Petchauer more than a decade ago. "Sometimes, Mike would have to get in his minivan and chase it for miles."

Petchauer died April 8 at age 51. Phinney had Dozer in his keeping by then. It played well with Jade. And it got along just fine with Phinney's wife, Tricia, and their kids.

Last Tuesday, Tricia forgot to lock the latch that held both dogs in their yard on Graceland Street NE. Phinney hopped into his vehicle and began searching.

He found his own dog, Jade, four houses away, and returned her to the yard.

Then he went looking for Dozer, a dog that "loved to run," and so Phinney had no idea how long his search might last.

He had never really gleaned details from Petchauer as to where Dozer's haunts might be. The dog could have gone anywhere.

But Dozer wasn't that far off, really. A distance of less than a mile. He headed south, and somehow survived either negotiating Monroe Avenue, or crossing Knapp and Ann streets, both busy thoroughfares.

But that's what it took for Dozer to return to the porch where he and his old friend shared time.

Phinney spotted the dog as he came around the corner. His heart soared to find the dog safe and sound. But it sank to know that there was no way he could communicate why Dozer's best friend left so suddenly. Dozer was barking at the front door, the moments spent out front, the view through the railing, maybe one more sunset. Dozer was missing Petchauer.

"I talked to him, and he whined back at me," said Phinney, "just like he was crying.

"I think he knows he's loved, but I wish he'd been human for just that moment, so he could understand."

Dancing Cheek to Cheek
is Daily Dream for EGR Couple

Too many of us are in a rush every morning: A hasty bagel, three swallows of java and a quick peck on the cheek.

Then there's Abe and Eileen Glaser, who start off each day cutting the rug.

OK, so it's ceramic tile. But how many couples do you know who begin each day by dancing in their kitchen?

It's a romantic ritual this East Grand Rapids couple has been performing for years, not only to celebrate the way they met, but to honor all the days of their lives.

Abe is nearly 90 and Eileen is 81. They are both on their second marriages, after losing spouses within weeks of each other about 23 years ago.

They met at a dance, where Abe proposed on the spot. Eileen remembers that "When I got into his arms, I told him I'd accept his proposal if he stopped smoking cigarettes."

Abe thought about it, and answered, "OK, but only if you'll stop putting two teaspoons of sugar into every cup of tea."

They wed six weeks later, in 1982.

Abe, who is retired from an auto salvage business on Grand Rapids' West Side, brought two grown children to the marriage. Eileen brought four.

She lost two others as toddlers – the first to complications from an accidental overdose of aspirin. The second developed a virus. Both boys were just 2 years old when they pulled them from her arms.

A relative eventually told Eileen that "You can grieve yourself into an institution. Or you can accept what can't be changed, and celebrate a daughter and three other healthy sons."

She ascended to the latter, and her friends will tell you that she is among the most positive people you ever will meet.

Eileen acknowledges that "hardly a day goes by that I don't try to compliment someone," and that can mean anyone from the clerk at the grocery store to a total stranger passing by.

"Both of us love people," Eileen says, "and we want to see people happy."

They set a sterling example.

Each morning, they rise around 7:30. Abe takes drops in his eyes, and Eileen downs a thyroid pill. Then it's back to bed for what Eileen calls "an hour of cuddling."

After making the bed, sharing breakfast and cleaning up the kitchen, they dance to CDs that generate music from yesteryear.

"We like Nat King Cole, Tony Bennet, Sinatra – all the greats," Abe says.

He leads, and she folds into his arms, tiptoeing at times to meet his embrace.

It is a very small dance floor, but neither seems to mind. He broke a hip last June; it doesn't show.

"Ah, 'Stardust,' " Abe says, and they slide and glide.

They will roam the kitchen for a half-hour, sometimes longer.

Between songs, they philosophize on where they are in their lives, and what has transpired. Their Jewish faith serves as a bulwark. And they have made friends in all corners.

"So many of the songs we play apply to our lives," says Eileen, nodding to both the tragedies and triumphs that affect us all.

They swing a bit to "Don't Get Around Much Anymore," which provides them with a workout without the hassle of an aerobics instructor.

Soon, they are settling again for something softer, and the kitchen quiets down.

"I want to tell you, I could just melt," Eileen says.

A little moment floats by. Abe draws her even closer.

He finally says, "Then melt."

Business Menu Offers
Warm Lesson on Life

You probably know the drill: Surround your world with upward climbers like yourself and plot strategies over a power lunch at some fancy restaurant.

Not for Tony Astras – a 50-year old insurance man who chose to entertain a close handful of colleagues at a most unlikely establishment.

His mother's house.

In truth, it is his mother's and father's house, but cancer claimed the patriarch of Tony's clan in December, when Stanley succumbed at the age of 83.

His death prompted Tony to assess his standing: Raising six children with his wife, Rita, but suddenly left with a mother who, at nearly 87, still had gifts to share.

When Tony's business associates – who meet monthly – came through the front door of the old home on Widdicomb Avenue NW this past Tuesday, Ursula Astras was fretting every detail.

She slept only two hours the night before, anxious over the luncheon now at hand.

More comfortable with her native Lithuanian tongue, she resorted to smiles and nods for Tony's guests: Susan Roeder, a special events production specialist; Dan Durkee, architect with Fishbeck, Thompson, Carr & Huber; Linda Beaumont, market research analyst with Bissell; Tom Crowley, owner of Kent Business Machines; and Jim Dieleman, president of Junior Achievement here.

Even before Tony could introduce them to his mother, the group was marveling at a home which is as much a museum as a place to raise a family.

"Unbelievable," said more than one visitor, inspecting the creations Ursula had fashioned from stalks of wheat.

"I remember the whole bathtub being full," Tony said, explaining how the wheat would have to be soaked before his mother would cut, slit and iron each sliver before backing them with tape and making three-dimensional works.

They also marveled at Ursula's etched eggs. Dozens of them grace the home.

So skilled is she in these Old World ways that Ursula has taught the craft at the Balzekas Museum of Lithuanian Culture in Chicago one Saturday a year for 30 years. Moreover, she has submitted her work to the Smithsonian Institute in Washington, D.C.

"Did you ever think when you were a little shepherd girl," Tony recalls asking her on the way to the nation's capital, "that you'd be invited by the most powerful country in the world to present your works?"

And the little shepherd girl certainly did not. She was born in Lithuania and fled during the Russian invasion more than 50 years ago.

Ursula was one of 12 children – six of whom died before they were 12. Like hundreds of other immigrants to Grand Rapids' West Side, they took up residence in the shadow of the American Seating Co., where Stanley methodically worked the lines.

Ursula raised Tony and his three siblings while scrubbing walls, preparing meals from scratch and doling out both love and discipline.

Tony also told a story about how he once wrote his parents to inform them that when they came to visit him at summer camp, he intended to go home with them. He waited with packed bags that Sunday afternoon. But to teach him a hard lesson in commitment and dedication, his folks simply didn't show.

If there is a tough side to Ursula – or Tony for that matter – it was dismissed roundly by the business group.

Instead, they focused in subtle ways on the relationship between Tony and his widowed mom and the strong, proud Lithuanian customs that help bind them.

"It's just so very tender, so very touching," said Susan Roeder, between bites of a potato cake called "kugelis," and a farmer's cheese with caraway seeds – both the product of Ursula's little kitchen.

The menu also included a cold beet soup, kielbasa with sauerkraut, and home-baked pastries.

Before the guests left, Tony managed to explain the why behind his method this day. Through welling tears, he told how he struggled with his father's death and recognized that his mother would be gone one day, too.

Come see, Tony was telling his friends. And look how well she gives.

Tony Astras is a former Marine. But he was first his mother's son and, on this sunny day inside the home he was raised, he gently said so.

Love Blankets Youngster's Life Unconditionally

We all have our crutches, but 10-year-old Sarah's is a threadbare rag of a former blanket. So you might have excused her father for saying "No" when she begged him to drive 135 miles to retrieve it from where they'd been vacationing.

Even more so when you consider that John, Sarah's dad, supervises a team of nearly 40 engineers working in Arizona at one of the nation's largest nuclear-energy plants. It is the sort of job for which vacations were invented in the first place.

I hooked up with Sarah and her family as they were making their way around Michigan, visiting long-time friends and relatives over a three-week period.

They agreed to relate the history of Sarah's blanket, which she calls her "bookie," provided I lose their last name. She is, after all, 10.

It was handed down to her from older brother Jeff, who "never really bonded with it," said Sarah's mother, Nancy. "It was still like brand new, and Sarah was a thumb sucker, and she'd hold it tight under her nose."

"For a while," Nancy remembered, "I could steal it away before she noticed it gone. But then, the more love it got, it aged, it weathered, and a lot of holes developed.

""Before long, we were tying knots in it just to keep it from falling apart." Everywhere that Sarah went, the bookie was sure to go. When I asked her what states it had traveled to, she rattled off "Wyoming, California, Utah, Michigan, New Mexico, Colorado, South Dakota, Ohio."

She is only mildly embarrassed to discuss it. Maybe because she knows of other girls her age with the same kind of attachment to similar huggables.

When Sarah enjoys sleep-overs at her friend Sheila's house, for instance, Sarah knows that Sheila sleeps with a baby blanket, too.

Though they don't discuss it between themselves, "She knows I have one, and I know she has one," says Sarah. "Some of the other girls have stuffed animals they bring, from when they were babies."

Bookie hasn't always been so treasured an item. When Sarah was 2 or 3, she wrapped a strand of her blanket around a tooth, and accidentally yanked it out, nearly root and all. Bookie can bring good luck, though: When the accident occurred, Sarah was visiting her uncle, who's a dentist.

At her home in Arizona, Sarah keeps her bookie on her bed, behind a pillow. When she travels, it belongs inside a pillow case, until it's time for slumber, when she's then allowed to remove it and cradle it in her hands.

Maybe you are wondering if Sarah has other special needs. She doesn't. A typical 5th-grader-to-be, she has lots of friends and is well-adjusted to school, where she earns fine grades. She competes in two sports. She is learning to play piano.

It's just that she has this bookie, and earlier this month, while staying at a cottage on Big Star Lake near Baldwin, she lost it there.

By the time she and her family had traveled nearly 70 miles to visit other friends near Muskegon, Sarah's mother was thinking to herself, "Maybe it's time to give it up."

But Sarah asked her father if he'd mind driving back to Lake County for one more look. Be it manipulative, or just one last earnest plea, she looked at him and said, "I'd do it for you."

But John already had decided he would go back, and he did find it, wedged between two mattresses. "I knew that it meant a lot to her," John would explain later. "You just do that for your kids."

No, every dad doesn't. Other dads make excuses, or might lie and say, "It was stolen," or get angry and tell their children to grow up.

Other parents, and they are everywhere, prop their feet up in lawn chairs and rationalize that 135 miles is way too far for some shriveled up baby blanket. Tell themselves, "Hey, this is MY vacation; let her tough it out."

But this dad didn't. On a gorgeous day made for lounging, he got back in the car and spent three hours in pursuit of a 10-year-old string of knots.

His wife, rather than exploring some other strategy, allowed him to make the drive. An older brother got a close-up lesson in unconditional love. And in a frayed, fragile world that is unraveling some itself, a little girl got a good night's sleep.

'They're together again'

LOWELL – The official cause of death for Willis "Ish" Hatch will be linked to an auto accident.

But if friends and relatives could pen the death certificate, they might enter just two words:

"Broken heart."

"I think we all feel that way," said Sandie VanWeelven, a close friend to the Hatches. Hatch, 92, died Tuesday evening, three days after pulling his vehicle into the path of another car in an accident that claimed the life of his wife, Arlene, 93.

A front-page column in Tuesday's Press quoted Willis Hatch mourning the loss of a woman with whom he fell asleep every night for 57 years after gazing at their special star.

The accident injured the driver of the other car as well – Katherine Tissue, 26, of Sydney, in Montcalm County, who suffered a broken foot. Her son, Cody, 4, escaped unhurt.

Hatch was admitted to Spectrum Health Butterworth Campus on Saturday with fractures to his pelvis and other complications. Relatives say he went into cardiac arrest around 6 p.m. Monday and died about 24 hours later.

"It's really tragic, but you know, it's for the best," VanWeelven said of his passing. Of his wife's death and his role in the accident, he "just couldn't be consoled," she said.

"We feel, completely, that this was a broken heart."

The couple lived most of their lives together on an 1800s-era farm near Alto. She taught in the Lowell schools for 33 years while he tended to cattle on what once was 300 acres.

Their presence in the Lowell-Alto community will be missed, friends said. They went everywhere together, often while holding hands. Stories of their sweetness and generosity surfaced throughout both towns in the wake of their deaths.

"Every time I saw Arlene," said Debra Hoeksema, who calls herself one of Hatch's unofficial grandkids, "she would grab my hand and hold it while we were talking. Both of these people had a huge impact not only on my life, but the lives of many others."

"When I graduated from high school, I went to their house to deliver my thank-you note for my graduation gift," recalled Sarah Larson. "I remember Arlene telling me she had something to show me. She quickly pulled out a letter that I had written them in elementary school to thank them for paying my way to church camp.

"Until she showed me the letter, I did not remember that they had done that for me. They were truly outstanding people, and they will be greatly missed."

Joan Vander Ziel, who with husband, Steve, lives just across the field from the Hatch place, echoed the sentiments of others when she figured that, "As of last night, (Ish) was with Arlene again looking at 'their star,' just from a closer vantage point."

Said nephew Mike Behler, following his uncle's death: "They're together again."

Hubby Showers Wife with Romantic Attention

Multiple Choice Quandry: It's Monday morning and your wife needs to shower, but the hot water heater is on the fritz. As a thoughtful husband, you:

A. Inform her that cold water is a great fat-burner.

B. Ship her off to the nearest KOA campground.

C. Tell her she doesn't smell that bad.

D. Get up at 4:30 a.m. to spend 90 minutes boiling water on the stove so she can enjoy a sumptuous bubble bath.

If you picked A or B or C, you are a lot like me.

If you picked D – and actually engaged in such romantic behavior – you might be winging your way to Hawaii soon.

Just like Bill and Kimberly Simpson of Stanton.

The Montcalm County couple won a trip to the Aloha State when Kimberly nominated her warm-hearted hubby for Woman's Day magazine's "Most Romantic Husband" contest – and won.

Her essay was picked as grand champion among 4,000 entries.

"It had our editors gushing," related Shavonne Harding, a spokeswoman for the weekly periodical, which treats its 21 million readers to a cameo about Bill and Kimberly in its Feb. 15 issue.

"He goes out of his way to show me, in little ways and in big ways, that he loves me," Kimberly says of her modern-day Romeo. "He opens doors for me. He sends me flowers for no reason. He makes every day a special occasion."

On the day Bill proposed marriage, he got down on bended knee in front of nearly 40 guests at a party he threw to celebrate Kimberly's graduation from college, then presented her a key. "You've got the key to my heart," he said, then popped the question.

On a weekend last winter, the couple woke up to a malfunctioning hot water heater. Unable to fix it immediately – and aware that his schoolteacher wife loved a morning shower or bath – Bill rose well before dawn and began boiling water on their electric stove, using virtually every pot and pan they owned, even their roaster.

"That bath was the most romantic thing ever!" Kimberly wrote in her essay to Woman's Day. "Bill was completely selfless, and the warm bath was perfect on a cold winter day."

"To me, it just seemed like a nice thing to do," says Bill, who spent five years as a political staffer at the state and national levels before teaming with his father to operate the Simpson Family Funeral Homes in Stanton and Sheridan. "I didn't think it was that big of a thing."

Kimberly did, though, and unbeknownst to her husband, mailed her essay. The magazine informed them of the win in October. This spring, they will bask in Hawaii's sunshine.

Skeptics might argue that Bill, 28 and Kimberly, 26, have only been married 14 months, and that when their honeymoon is over, acts like drawing a hot bath from the stove will fade.

No way, says Kimberly. "He's the most-caring guy ever."

You won't find any argument from Jan Seaver. She owns the "Chat & Chew Cafe" three miles down the road in Sheridan. "Billy is a town favorite," she said of the young man she has known since he was a tot. "Did he tell you that?"

According to Seaver, 'Billy' "is a very loving and caring man," and of his bathtub bravado, she said, "I can imagine him doing that. I don't care if you're 3 years old or 109, he's kind to people."

Seaver was so impressed with the announcement by Woman's Day that she blew up the picture and posted it in her eatery.

Longtime pal Dan Petersen offered some good-natured ribbing. "We've got a Super Bowl party coming up this Sunday and we haven't hung around together since the magazine came out," said Petersen. "So I can tell you this: The Eagles won't be the only ones getting beat up that day."

As for the rest of us guys who think being romantic means remembering to keep the toilet seat down, we can make fun of Cupids like Bill Simpson all we want, but he'll have the last laugh at a luau.

"Some of my buddies have been giving me kind of a rough time," Bill acknowledges. "I'll just add 'em to my list of 'Wish-you-were-here-in-Hawaii' postcards."

Son's Love Soars on Angels' Wings

Anyone who witnessed the spectacular takeoff last Monday of an F/A-18 Hornet from Gerald R. Ford International Airport might have dismissed it as just another gung-ho flyboy anxious to impress his friends.

Hardly so. It was a member of the U.S. Navy's elite Blue Angels precision flying team – and a Grand Rapids native at that – saluting his mother for what might have been the last time.

Mazie Boogerd has liver cancer and is not expected to improve. Her son, Chip, recently was named a member of the Blue Angels. Last week, he flew his Navy jet from Pensacola to Grand Rapids to celebrate Easter. When he left on Monday, he arranged to bid his mother a bittersweet farewell with an aerial tribute that rocked the skies over southern Kent County.

"He conveyed to us that he was going to do a fly-by," said Mazie's husband, Bart. "I told him, 'We'll be there.'"

Bart, 62, operates an accounting concern. His wife of 41 years, who's 61, directed a business called Closets Etc. before taking sick. Together, they've raised four children, and like any clan, they endured the roller coaster that is life. They have family photos that render youth as a glorious time, and scores of other pictures that paint a portrait of a family in constant flux. Together, they laughed, they cried, they survived.

These days, though, the ride is laborious and painful. Three years ago, Mazie was diagnosed with colon cancer. Though treatments initially proved hopeful, the cancer eventually spread to her liver, where a tumor is now lodged. "We take each day one day at a time," says a tearful Bart.

Mazie draws a deep breath and cries. "I think," she says through her own tears, "that it was the most difficult thing I've ever done."

But she wasn't referring directly to her illness. Instead she meant realizing that Monday's farewell might have been the last. Because of the Blue Angels' rigorous demonstration schedule, Chip is permitted just two weekends off every six months. Though the Angels are set to perform July 1-2 in Traverse City, he's not expected to have any more formal free time until August.

The oldest of the four children, Lt. Cmdr. Chip Boogerd graduated in 1982 from Grand Rapids Christian High School, and later from Western Michigan University, with a degree in aviation technology.

He is 36 years old with a wife, Geri, and two daughters, Ansley, nearly 4, and Jordan, not yet 2.

Ever since he was a little boy spilling out of the house to watch planes go overhead, Chip Boogerd had wanted to be a pilot.

"I worked at Northern Air," he said of the facility at the airport here, "and I fell in love with aviation."

Ascending to the position of a Navy Blue Angel is next to impossible. The Holy Grail. "My earliest recollection of them is at an air show in Kalamazoo," Boogerd says. "But it was too lofty a dream then."

A Blue Angel show cannot be described in words. In planes capable of reaching 1,320 miles per hour, or nearly twice the speed of sound, pilots put on demonstrations that are the epitome of precision and daring. At times, the aircraft are a mere 18 inches apart as they roar overhead.

On the day Chip arrived here, his mother was so weak, she couldn't attend. But by Monday, she'd found a reserve, and Bart drove her to the airport.

When a Hornet aircraft is on the premises, word gets around, and by the 2:15 p.m. takeoff time, small crowds were gathering near the runway.

Before walking to his plane, Chip told his mother that he loved her and that he thought of her constantly. He embraced her as she sat in the family car. It was not an easy thing for him or for her, when he turned and strode off.

Chip had filed a flight plan with the tower that would take him to Pensacola at an altitude of just over 40,000 feet, and put him there in less than two hours. But he had requested something on behalf of his mother as well, and somehow, Mazie was finding the strength to exit the car and make her way in Bart's arms to a chain-link fence that rimmed the runway.

So impressive was the sight of Boogerd's Hornet awaiting takeoff, that a large commercial jet in line ahead of him volunteered to let Boogerd have the honors. "We accede to the Navy's Blue Angel," radioed the pilot of the larger plane.

With Mazie still embraced in her husband's arms, Chip finished taxiing, then burst down the runway and lifted off. It was an impressive sight, but he wasn't finished yet.

When he was but a blue speck in the distance, he banked right and started back to perform a fly-by. When he leveled off and tipped his wings for his mother, he was screaming at nearly 600 mph, with afterburners engaged.

"We got a couple of noise complaints," said John Converse, assistant air traffic manager. "People around here are used to hearing noise, but not those afterburners. They were pretty understanding when they heard the explanation, though."

The roar and vibration were nothing compared to Chip Boogerd's final display. Immediately after bursting past his parents, he broke into a vertical ascent, and at nearly 500 feet per second, rocketed straight up into the heavens, disappearing even into a cloudless sky.

Necks craned. People gasped. Heads shook in awe. And as Chip Boogerd continued to power up, unfurling both his wings and his love, a tiny figure below waved goodbye to her Blue Angel.

Acknowledgements

I've had a lot of wind at my back over a newspaper career that spanned nearly 31 years, mostly comprised of all the people who opened their doors to me when I came knocking for a story.

Years before that, though, were teachers who emphasized the importance of accuracy and imagery in writing, and they peppered my way through St. James Catholic elementary school, West Catholic High, Grand Rapids Community College, Alma College and Grand Valley State University. Among the best were Walt Lockwood and the late Marinus Swets, both of GRCC.

Two colleagues, both of whom died too young, inspired me to see beyond surfaces. I will always be indebted to Corky Meinecke and Jim Mencarelli for setting the bar high.

At The Press, I worked alongside countless editors who often made my stuff much better than what I'd initially submitted. A very partial list includes John Barnes, Jeff Cranson, Andy Angelo, Peg West, Ruth Butler, Julie Hoogland, Tanda Gmiter, Tom Nowak, Scott Langford, Ben Beversluis and all the others who put their talented fingerprints on my work.

I found encouragement at virtually every turn from fellow reporters, photographers, editors and others who became lifelong friends.

My family belongs here for what they had to put up with when I'd be fighting a deadline with nothing in the crosshairs, and for taking it in stride when they became the target. Thank-you Hollie and Tom, Patrick and Andrew.

I owe a tremendous debt of gratitude to Press Publisher Danny Gaydou, who so graciously gave me the green light to publish this book.

For the expert design and photography that make this book and its cover sing, I thank Gregg Palazzolo and Ben Benefiel at PalazzoloDesign.com in Ada, as well as Robert Neumann of The Big Event photo studio in Grand Rapids.

Finally, I am grateful to retired Press Editor Mike Lloyd, who took a gamble back in 1978 and hired me – fresh out of college with degrees in special education and psychology – as part of his fledgling staff at The Press. I told him I would sweep floors to get my foot in the door. He put a pen in my hand instead. I have been splitting wood since.

For More Information
on Author Tom Rademacher
and "Splitting Wood:"

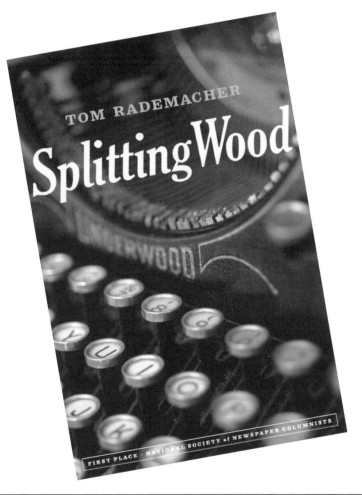

To post a comment, explore bulk pricing, order books by mail,
or schedule Tom Rademacher for a presentation to your class
or group, visit: TomRademacheronline.com